# Take a Stand

# Take a Stand

## Successful Traits of Female Leaders

Kelly Murray Spivey

ROWMAN & LITTLEFIELD
*Lanham • Boulder • New York • London*

Published by Rowman & Littlefield
An imprint of The Rowman & Littlefield Publishing Group, Inc.
4501 Forbes Boulevard, Suite 200, Lanham, Maryland 20706
www.rowman.com

86-90 Paul Street, London EC2A 4NE, United Kingdom

British Library Cataloguing in Publication Information Available

**Library of Congress Cataloging-in-Publication Data**

Names: Spivey, Kelly Murray, 1963– author.
Title: Take a stand: successful traits of female leaders / Kelly
     Murray Spivey.
Description: Lanham, MD: Rowman & Littlefield : School
     Superintendents Association, [2022] | Summary: "After reading
     this book more women will gain the confidence necessary to
     apply for executive positions and feel safe to openly discuss
     discrepancies when they occur."—Provided by publisher.
Identifiers: LCCN 2021061719 (print) | LCCN 2021061720 (ebook) |
     ISBN 9781475863888 (cloth) | ISBN 9781475863895 (paperback) |
     ISBN 9781475863901 (epub)
Subjects: LCSH: Women executives. | Leadership in women. |
     Executive ability.
Classification: LCC HD6054.3 .S774 2022 (print) | LCC HD6054.3
     (ebook) | DDC 658.4/09082—dc23/eng/20220112
LC record available at https://lccn.loc.gov/2021061719
LC ebook record available at https://lccn.loc.gov/2021061720

# Contents

# Preface

As the granddaughter, daughter, sister, mother, and grandmother of a long line of strong women, it is important to share the personal experiences as a female leader within the workforce. My great grandmother was the first female postmaster on a rural mountain in Georgia. My mother was born to a country singer, Fairley Holden, who achieved only a fourth grade education. She was the first in her family to receive a college degree. Her mother was a house cleaner but always earned enough money to take care of their needs. She displayed the value of education to her children.

I was taught at a young age that men are the head of the household, however; women can be and achieve anything in life. I had strong, loving, determined, and supportive parents. I knew by third grade that I would be a teacher. I knew by high school that I wanted to be an elementary principal. Early in my career, in my second year of teaching, I began my master's program as I aspired to be a superintendent.

After I taught school for a few years, my husband and I decided to start our family. I learned over the holiday break that we were expecting our first child. When I returned to work to share the news with the staff and my administrator, I was taken a bit back. Although the staff was excited to celebrate this new event, the male administrator didn't mince words when he informed me that I was lucky that I could still work. After all, it was just a few decades ago that women couldn't teach if they were expecting a child. I was floored by this news and couldn't wait to share his response with my mother who was also an administrator. She confirmed that this information was true. In 1962–1963, she learned that she was carrying her second child. As a full time teacher, she decided not to share this news within anyone outside the family because she feared losing her job. She and my father depended on this income and knew that her job would be in jeopardy if this announcement came too early.

This historical workplace practice came as a total surprise. Who would ever think that women stopped working because they were expecting a child? How can this practice occur within a profession that is all about the child, student? Do men stop working when their wife is expecting a child? Why did such a mindset ever get established? Where were the equality rights during this time period? Although I didn't have my first child until 1987 and only took a six-week maternity leave, why was this conversation still occurring within the workplace? Did this kind of questioning guilt mothers to stay home with their children?

In 1992, after teaching seven years, I became an assistant principal in a wealthy suburban district. As I was learning new routines, procedures, expectations, and developing relationships, I was surprised about the interactions among the administrative team members. The dynamics of the group involved eight males and four females. The meeting was called to solve one district issue. I learned quickly there was an unspoken process. When a male central office leader proposed a problem, it was time for the entire administrative team to brainstorm possible solutions. Quickly, a female and non-white principal provided a possible solution. In my opinion, it was a great option to solve the problem. I was a bit surprised when no one responded to the proposal. Matter of fact, it was skipped over with no discussion. Forty-five minutes later, a male provided the same solution as the female had earlier in the meeting. It was then that the group began providing feedback to his suggested plan of action.

This experience as a young female leader was very eye opening for me. Why were there fewer females at the table? Were females being treated the same? I knew of the research behind gender expectations within the classroom. I never really thought about this possibly being displayed in the workplace among adults. When I later reflected upon this experience with another female administrator, we admired the problem, laughed about the situation, and made excuses for the behavior of the group. Not once did we ever suggest ways to address the unspoken problem, the elephant in the room. The problem was definitely admired with *no* solution. It was obviously an accepted condition. Now, I realize that when women accept the unspoken conditions taking place in the executive boardroom, we are perpetuating the problem.

The next phase in my career was an elementary principal where the majority of elementary administrators were female. Although there wasn't a male dominance within the organization, I was reminded that women are often competitive and fall into the "Queen Bee Syndrome." This is where there is little support for one another and there is definitely a hierarchy within the order. As a female, if this condition weren't accepted, one would easily experience negative behaviors from their peers.

During the next eight years served in education, I was an assistant superintendent. My years in this position were focused on student learning. There was no time to pay attention to what I perceived as "gender games" within the workplace. I enjoyed the relationships and valued the experience. However, there was so much work to focus on that my motto was to keep the lens on the students. The last seven years of my thirty-three years in education, I served as a superintendent. I never gave much thought that there was only one other female superintendent in the county or that I was the first female superintendent that served longer than 1.5 years in the district. It wasn't until I began meeting with other superintendents across the state when I learned that 17% of the superintendents were female in the state where I served and 24% in the nation. I began to look around the leadership table in my own district and found that I had more men than women. How did this happen? I was responsible for the hiring and didn't pay attention to the gender outcome. If I want to see change, I can't expect it to start at the state level, it needs to start at home.

Another light bulb effect was that when I participated at the state or national level in my executive role, I found myself accepting the same thing, female responses not appearing as valued as the male responses when problem solving. Without thought I also began implementing strategies that gave others credit or made it appear that the suggested ideas were coming from someone else. This was how the work got done and that is all that mattered.

It wasn't until I retired that I really spent time in this reflection. Why did I feel that the work wouldn't get done if it came from a female? Why did I feel it was necessary to make the idea appear to be from my male counterpart? I have two daughters, two granddaughters, and two grandsons. Change needs to happen now.

Do I want to model such beliefs, attitudes, and mindsets to them? Do young girls learn how to manipulate to survive? Are we taught the behaviors to appear less confident or superior? Are these attitudes, behaviors, and mindsets innate or learned? How do we change this paradigm for our daughters and granddaughters? What habits or characteristics do female executive women have in common? This began the journey of much reflection. I soon realized that this wasn't just a journey for women; it is one that isn't gender specific.

I found writing this book extremely therapeutic. Although I didn't have time in my personal work journey to understand the rationale of how women and men work and process differently in the workplace, I found the research thereafter to be rewarding. After reading this book, I hope that others join this important journey in changing the paradigm for women. May more purposeful decisions and goals pertaining to personal careers be made so that more women will achieve individual understanding and professional success.

# Acknowledgments

Although this book is written from my personal experience, I believe that there is information that will resonate with others. I've had the benefit of working with many people in my thirty-three-plus years served in education; however, the most gratitude is extended to my husband, Terry, who is my biggest supporter. Although my parents raised me the first twenty years, Terry is responsible for refining me. He always encourages me to be better and to never hold back, while he works and takes care of the family. He is an active listener and never hesitates to question my actions, causing me to constantly reflect upon my practice and decision making. He pushes me to be a stronger person and to be the best I can be.

I thank my mother and sisters, who share this wonderful profession and serve with great passion. They are consistent sounding boards. I'm so grateful for my two daughters, who are strong, independent women. They use their voice to make active change, displaying a fearless attitude in standing up for the underdogs of the world. They give me hope that their generation will do a better job of addressing biases and make this a better world.

A special thank you goes to Dr. Nancy Finkle Wagner, a member of my female tribe, a dear friend, and a colleague. She spent much time reviewing the content of this book and challenging my thinking. It would be neglectful to forget my coworkers and workshop participants who I've worked with throughout the years. I appreciate their open, honest input about their experiences and ways to improve our craft. It has been very rewarding to work with such great people. Thank you.

# Introduction

*Take a Stand* is written for all of the women who aspire to achieve great things but don't have the confidence to make the leap forward. There are experiences throughout life that are learned and some that we, as females, even perpetuate. These experiences contribute to the established attitudes, behaviors, and mindsets, which may hold some females back. It is time to create awareness and understanding and share personal learning and stories among our peers so that appropriate change within the culture and workplace can become systemic.

Those who have read the book *Men Are from Mars and Women Are from Venus* quickly learned that men and women communicate and process information much differently. This information is enlightening for couples to learn. It makes the opposite sex understand that there are times when their partner may appear to be disconnected or uncaring but that's not always the case.

In the work environment, this information can also be helpful in understanding how men and women make decisions differently. Do you ever think that men can be bullies or that women can appear too soft in the workplace? Rather than critically judge one another, it is important for opposite genders to understand such differences to have the most impact on an organization.

This understanding isn't just important for opposite sexes; it is also crucial for women to understand their own behavior toward other women. Have you ever wondered why women complain about other women in the work environment? Rather than build one another up or find a strong candidate to mentor as the next leader, women can oftentimes be seen talking behind one another's backs. This must be corrected if it occurs. No one grows their individual talents in a toxic environment.

Healthy work environments engage all workers in defining the purpose and mission of the organization and working toward a common understanding of positive relationships, mindsets, and attitudes.

Women are frequently underrepresented in executive positions. The few that secure such positions are often paid less than their male counterparts. It is time for women to acknowledge such disparities and begin supporting one another in personal and professional growth. It is also key for everyone to understand gender differences in communication, processing, and problem solving to become more supportive and use the information to achieve optimal success.

After reading *Take a Stand*, it is hoped that more women will gain the confidence necessary to apply for executive positions and feel safe in openly discussing discrepancies when they occur. Moreover, this book is written to encourage reflection about where women have been, where they are today, and where they are headed. It is time to stand up and make the necessary changes for the future.

# PART I

# Successful Leaders Know Where They've Been

# Chapter 1

# Historical Overview

The beginning is always today.—Mary Wollstonecraft

*Personal Story*

*My paternal grandmother, Myrtle Murray, was born in 1898 on a tobacco farm in the hills of Kentucky. Her house didn't have indoor plumbing, electricity, or running water. Her mother, Great Grandma Lavaca McDaniel, raised the last several of her seventeen children on her own because her husband died of a gunshot wound when my grandmother was only three years old.*

*I would often stop by her house as a young adult to ask her questions about her lifetime. I found it amazing to learn about her primitive young life. When she was young, she really did walk a few miles to and from school. She wore the shoes and clothes from her older siblings. Rarely was anything new. Often the girls would only attend school until the eighth grade while the boys would attend through high school. My grandmother shared that many times the girls were needed in the home to help grow crops, farm the animals, cook, and clean.*

*When she was fifteen years old, she married and left home. This was before women were allowed to vote. She had her first child at age sixteen and her last at age forty-two. She never thought about attending high school or college because the expectation was that women became wives and mothers.*

*Myrtle lived through the innovation of cars, radios, television, saw the first man walk on the moon, and the invention of computers. She and her husband owned their own successful business.*

*Myrtle's middle daughter was a "Rosie the Riveter," one of the females replacing males in their industrial position during World War II, never earning the equal pay as the male worker.*

*It is unimaginable that two generations before me didn't have the right to vote. The right to vote was only granted to the white men who were in charge of writing legislation.*

*My grandmother was only twenty-two years old when the 19th Amendment of the United States Constitution was ratified, stating, "The right of citizens of the United States to vote shall not be denied or abridged by the United States or by any State on account of sex."*

*It is important to understand how this information creates awareness and understanding. Gender disparity has occurred for hundreds of years. Is status quo enough? This question can only be answered within each individual.*

History states that the "Age of Enlightenment" occurred in about 1650 in Europe. During that time, there was chatter surrounding the idea that women were as competent as men. More than a hundred years later, women began to gradually enter the workforce. In the 1820s, men began to unionize for more pay and shorter workdays. It wasn't until the 1920s that women became part of the Federal Department of Labor. Although the passage of the Civil Rights Act of 1964 increased the power of the women in the workforce, the wages of equal jobs between male and female have never been equivalent.

In the early 1970s, women continued to fight for equal rights. In 1971, songwriter Helen Reddy wrote her first hit. The first time her song was pitched to a producer, her lyrics weren't supported because they were too controversial. The producer was adamant about not supporting the women's liberation movement. That same year, Helen received a Grammy for her forever-remembered song, "I Am Woman."

In the 1980s, the Reagan era, the women's movement entered a new phase. At the 1984 Democratic Convention, Geraldine Ferraro became the first female to be nominated for vice president by a large political party. Even television showcased women in the workplace as supporting their families and themselves, while speaking out for women's rights and equality. Two TV shows, *Family Ties* and *The Cosby Show*, starred strong, working female leads. Although this era was characterized by some advancement, it was also a time of much backlash.

From the 1950s to the 1990s, data indicates that there was a 9% increase in women leaders in state and federal leadership positions. Today, there are approximately 27% of women in state and federal leadership positions. There were great strides made in cultural feminism in the 1990s. The "Girl Power" movement promised that progress for women would trickle down to girls, too.

In the early 2000s, women activism moved at a faster rate due to the advancement of cell phones. Since 2010, social media outlets have activated a larger movement. Women are sharing more stories and leading marches, and they have created the Me Too Movement.

Although many women have fought for hundreds of years to gain equal rights, today 76% of those in education are women but only 25% of them are superintendents serving school districts in the United States. This percentage has increased approximately 7% in the past fifteen years. According to demographic studies, this percentage has doubled since the year 2000. This figure is similar to those for other executive positions in other organizations, for example, doctors, lawyers, CEOs, and so forth.

If gender disparity outcomes are to change, there needs to be a change in the workplace, at home, and in school culture. It certainly isn't a result of competence that only 25% of women versus 75% of men are currently serving in executive educational positions.

It is time to stand up, speak the truth, question inappropriate behavior, and educate one another to become more aware and learn effective strategies for change. If we continue to ignore and fail to acknowledge that certain behaviors exist that perpetuate this problem, minimal change will continue to occur. It is time to actively change this paradigm.

It is also time for everyone to understand the importance of shaping young girls into confident, strong, and loving women. We need to teach young girls that using their voice to fight for improvement in the world isn't being loud and bossy, it is actually a wonderful leadership quality. It is up to adults to mold our young children into good listeners, positive thinkers, and innovative problem solvers. It is time to shape attitudes, behaviors, and mindsets differently so that young girls can gain the confidence necessary to adequately compete with the males in the workplace.

It is important for the reader to understand that this book ISN'T about men versus women or that women are superior to men. It is designed for reflection, causing one to ask, "Am I pleased with the outcome of the number of women in executive positions?" If not, then what can individuals do to impact change? How do people within their personal circles and/or workplace encourage young girls and women to be natural leaders and not to accept the status quo that exists today?

In summary, there is a need to elevate women to power in public education and other executive roles. It is time for women to stand up and be empowered to take charge of their own destiny. To begin pursuing job advancements of interest and not wait to be asked to interview. It's time for women to make strong decisions for the issue of gender disparity not to perpetuate.

Women need to support one another and encourage other females to use their voice to have a candid conversation about the topic. This work will become easier once there is an awareness and understanding of the differences and why these differences occur. Moving forward with a growth mindset will allow us to collaborate and identify strategies to make women more confident and effective in executive roles.

## PROBLEM-SOLVING SCENARIO

During the first year serving as (the first female) superintendent of the "Unknown School District," an eye-opening experience occurs at a home football game. The weather quickly turns to a potential threat. Dark clouds and high winds move in quickly. According to a weather app, tornado-like conditions are developing. A decision about the game needs to be made quickly.

The home superintendent approaches the opposing district's male superintendent, who has a somewhat arrogant facial expression. Stepping out of the hurdle to make a formal introduction, extending out a hand with a smile and introduction, the female superintendent welcomes the male superintendent to the school district as she begins to express her concern about the threatening weather. The opposing superintendent ignored the gesture and kept walking. For a second, the rude behavior was acknowledged before rejoining the huddle to discuss an action plan.

As the host of the home game, a suggestion is made to move players into the locker rooms and participants into the gym for safety. As the other (male) superintendent, guest to the home site, ignored all dialogue, the athletic director was directed to implement the emergency hazardous plan. If nothing else, the evacuation would make a great practice exercise for the books and keep the participants safe. Once the football field was evacuated, the officials called the game and rescheduled it for the following night.

The car ride home is very interesting for the home superintendent. Everyone in the car acknowledged that the male superintendent would have never ignored another male superintendent. It was agreed that his behavior and attitude were definite examples of gender discrepancy in the workplace. It was obvious that the male superintendent from the opposing team didn't think that the superintendent position was a job for females.

## Questions

1. Should the female superintendent address the male superintendent about his inappropriate behavior? If so, what is gained from this? If not, when would it be appropriate to address?

## Reflections

- Can you think of a time in your personal or professional circumstances where gender roles differed? Was this a written rule or an unspoken rule? Did you seek clarity by engaging in a conversation or did you actively avoid it? Why?

# Chapter 2

# Fewer Females Are Promoted to Top Executive Leadership Positions

When you undervalue what you do, the world will undervalue you.—Oprah Winfrey

*Always the Maid of Honor, Never the Bride*

*I feel like I've been to several weddings dressed up as the maid of honor and never the bride. I've advanced to the top two superintendent candidates for openings in two different school districts. Each time, the position was appointed to the male. On one occasion, several of the community members in the selection process reported that I was the favorite choice by the community. In this very same district, another person reported that the position was always going to the male with the least amount of experience but well known by the board.*

*When people are involved in a process but aren't heard, trust is broken. At times this is irreparable. If a district knows who they want, they are better off appointing the candidate rather than involving the community in a process that is in name only.—Anonymous author*

Numerous reports indicate that women make up at least half of all employees in the workforce, yet only 25% make it to top executive positions. In Fortune 500 companies, only 5% of women are appointed to these top positions. In the fields of law and medicine, there are only 20% of women in such power positions. In the U.S. Congress, only 27% of females are elected to the state and federal leadership positions.

Questions for the reader:

1. Are you satisfied with these results?
2. Although the numbers have slightly increased over the past sixty years, is this enough movement toward equity?
3. Is there ever a time when one should be less active in moving this issue forward?
4. If not, why is there still a gap in the above statistics?

Data strongly indicates that females are less likely to receive promotions because males receive more encouragement, mentorships, and sponsorships, and that men make up the majority of people in the boardrooms making such decisions.

Some would express that less women are in the top roles because of stereotypical qualities, such as women can't do the work because of maternity leave and child care issues. Although such statements aren't legal, they continue to occur.

Others say that fewer women apply for the top executive positions because they lack confidence and don't feel that they possess 100% of the skill sets identified on the job description. There is research to support that young girls learn such attitudes, behaviors, and mindsets at an early age.

Research also indicates that women are often reported as the "top performers," yet are less likely to be promoted. When women do advance, research states that they make an average of 20% less than the men do. Gender bias still exists today and it continues to interfere with women receiving equal promotions or pay for equal work. If this is to change, women need to continue to be activists in the work.

To support this data several personal stories will be shared in this chapter to indicate the gender disparity still exists today. One story is about a famous actress, the second is about an attorney, the third is about experiences reported from several female educational leaders, and the last is about a gender bias experiment. All of the stories vary in time, but not results. They express similar experiences around gender disparity in top leadership positions.

Geena Davis, famous actress, spoke to a group of women leaders at a forum located at Miami University in Oxford, Ohio, in 2015. Ms. Davis spoke on this topic of gender disparity. She shared her experiences as an actress and the pay differences between the female and male leading actors in the film industry. During her experience, often the female lead actress would receive far less scenes and less pay than the male lead. This pay discrepancy continues to exist today.

Gender disparity isn't just found in one vocation. It occurs everywhere. During a flight to Los Angeles, a man on the plane began a conversation about his experiences as a former attorney. Although he had no idea of the author's personal experiences or interest in writing a book on beliefs, attitudes, and mindsets about female executives in the workplace, he had personal experience pertaining to this topic.

He reported that there were fewer practicing female attorneys, or judges, and that he found his female counterparts were treated differently within the courtroom and firm. This was visible from informal expectations of how to dress to the number of hours put into the work. He also reported that within his firm, it was his observation that females had to work twice as hard as the males to achieve partnership status. The conversation on the plane caused some reflection about the fact that there are far less female lawyers and judges as other leading positions across the nation.

An example of this scenario is also found in the Federal Supreme Court. For those that visit the Supreme Court, one would find the following words written above the main entrance: "EQUAL JUSTICE UNDER THE LAW." Today, there are nine Supreme Court justices, of which six are men and three are women. Thanks go to Ruth Bader Ginsburg, Associate Justice of the U.S. Supreme Court, who served from 1993 to 2020 and was known for her work on gender disparity. She was the second female justice appointed after Sandra Day O'Connor and the first Jewish woman.

Again, some gains have been made over the past several decades. However, to truly change oppression, the work can never stop. Some may feel that this is a strong statement; however, story after story continues to support that this work will never be done. Women continue to receive fewer promotions for the top executive positions and when they do, they receive significantly less salary.

Women leaders that interviewed for the top executive position in school districts often reported that they were selected as one of the top two candidates for the final interview. All of them reported that they were selected for the runner up to the finalist, who was the male candidate. The following captions and / or statements were noted in recent seminars across the state:

1. "I was told that I didn't get the position because I was too smart. They didn't want the employees to feel inferior."
2. "I was asked how I could do the job since I was a mother of several children."
3. "I felt like I didn't get the job because I wore a dress and not a pants suit."
4. "I was the token female that made it to the top two candidate forum when the rumor in the community was that the job was ALWAYS going to the male candidate with less experience. I believe they just needed a female to balance out the gender equity roles for the interview process."
5. "I was asked to take the advanced position because of my history in the community. Once I had the CEO position, I was asked why I had so many female leaders. This caused me to reflect. If this was a man in this position, would he ask why so many males work for him?"
6. "Why is it that when females retire from a superintendent position, the board will state that a male is needed because the previous superintendent was female?
7. "This occurs with young girls, too. My eleven-year-old daughter placed first in the state and third in the nation in a swimming event. One of the young boys on the swim team informed her that if she were a boy, she wouldn't have placed so highly with her time."

The last example of gender bias is found in one of the activities used in this training series. It is a video from an *ABC News* clip with Diane Sawyer. Although the video is old it still demonstrates results seen today. The video displays a male and female candidate using the same words when responding to the same interview question. The only difference was voice tone and nonverbal gestures. The male was observed as a proactive leader, while the woman was viewed as a bitchy boss.

Once the participants within this experiment saw the video clip of them interviewing candidates, yet viewing the same responses entirely different, they were shocked. It made the participants within the experiment understand that gender disparity is real. They even wondered if they had been the recipients of this in former interviews. Why is it that the female's tone or body language is viewed negatively when their verbal response is the same as the male? This should cause much reflection. What are children being taught? Are girls learning at a young age that they can't do what boys do? Are they being taught that they will never live up to boys' expectations?

Research does support that girls learn such attitudes, behavior, and mindsets at a very young age. There is also research to support that there are some psychological and physical differences. This means that how we go about a task may differ, but it doesn't mean that it can't be done.

The fear in this dialogue is that it is teaching our young girls that negative words, actions, and expectations are status quo. If this is the case, will girls ever have the confidence to be their best? When they are at their best and it is misperceived, does it really matter how they perform? This can set the state of the mindsets, behaviors, and attitudes of individuals.

Although there are laws about equality, practices don't always mirror the expectation. This could be due to unknown personal biases from those in charge of hiring; therefore, those in charge of hiring may benefit from bias training.

Differential pay among different genders continues to be a struggle. According to national data, there is one female superintendent to every three appointed male superintendents. Moreover, the 2020–2021 survey indicates that there is a discernible difference in salaries by gender, with males reporting higher base salaries. See table 2.1.

Table 2.1 indicates that women who have the executive position don't make equal pay for equal work. Salary discrepancy hasn't improved during the last several hundred years. Note: The same type of salary discrepancy is noted in top executive business positions.

**Table 2.1. Superintendent Base Salary**

| Gender | Minimum | 25% | Median | 75% | Maximum | N |
|---|---|---|---|---|---|---|
| Female | $65,000 | $106,275 | $127,961 | $170,000 | $223,000 | 375 |
| Male | $102,000 | $135,000 | $157,000 | $198,950 | $345,000 | |
| Prefer not to respond | $150,000 | $150,000 | $183,471 | $183,471 | $217,350 | 4 |
| Omitted | $150,000 | $150,000 | $150,000 | $216,000 | $428,000 | 17 |
| Total | | | | | | |

As a former female superintendent, salary negotiation became very difficult. The feeling was that the salary would equal performance and that justification was viewed as weak in nature. Today, salaries and benefits between males and females continue to be significantly different. Women need to be reassured that it is acceptable to negotiate for improved conditions, career advancement, and an increase in salaries at work. Individuals are responsible for personal growth and negotiation for themselves.

Women that are in top executive positions are known to have voiced an interest in the position early in their career. Expressing an interest in a position and sharing a plan of action is the key to success. Women in the top 5% of the 500 Clubs are seen as exceptional performers and aren't afraid to ask for the salary deserved. Studies indicate that men do a much better job negotiating their salary than women. Women tend to think salary equals performance and if it isn't immediate, it will come with time and results.

Women need to be reminded that when entering the field, the negotiated salary sets the stage for the future. It is important to negotiate hard in the beginning. This would be a great topic for mentors to talk over with the person they are training for a future job. This is certainly a skill taught, not learned.

In summary, statistics continue to report that there are numerous examples of inequality among genders in the workforce. Although improvement has been made, significant changes still need to occur for male and females to be equal in top executive roles and pay. This information shouldn't be paralyzing. Hopefully, it encourages women to advocate for themselves when seeking job advancements and negotiating salary.

It is important for women to have a career plan, network, seek a sponsor, and confidently apply for the top executive positions. Once the job is offered, women need to certainly advocate for the pay deserved based on experience and comparability salary reports.

## PROBLEM-SOLVING SCENARIO

You have been a female math teacher in the local high school for the past ten years. You recently received your license to be a school administrator. At the end of the school year, you learn of a new second-ary administrator vacancy in your district. You served as a department chair in your building and served on a district committee with the superintendent. However, when you view the job description, you don't feel that you are qualified. When your male counterpart views the job description, he feels confident that he is ready to apply for the administrative position, although he didn't serve in such leadership capacities.

## Questions

1. Why does the female teacher not feel adequate to apply for the position?
2. Why does the male teacher feel adequate to apply for the position?
3. If on the interview committee, which candidate would you select to interview? Why?

## Reflections

- Have you been part of an interview committee where a male and female candidate were the top two candidates for the position? If so, who got the job? Why?
- Did the organization committee use a gender bias instrument?
- Can you think of a time in your professional career where males and females were paid differently for the same job? If so, how would you address the issue?

# Chapter 3

# Queen Bee Syndrome

If you judge people, you have no time to love them.—Mother Teresa

*Queen Bee*

*The ultimate queen bee is a woman who makes it to the top of her profession but refuses to help other women reach the same heights. Does this sound familiar?*

*The author of this story describes a terrible work environment when sharing that her female boss treated her much differently than her colleagues once she became aware that she had a master's degree and could be in direct competition for future promotions.*

*The boss was somewhat nice to her face but would often put her down in front of other colleagues, making them doubt her true value and overall effectiveness. These inappropriate remarks made the boss appear superior.*

*Have you ever heard the phrase, "May the best person get the job"? People can usually see through false accusations and unprofessional words. It is never appropriate for a boss to discuss another employee's performance in front of other colleagues.—Anonymous author*

Have you ever asked yourself, "Who would I rather work for, a man or a woman"? Many females often respond that they prefer working for a man, but they complain when top-performing females are passed over for job advancements. This causes much reflection. Do women really support other women in the workplace? Are women more competitive with other women? Are women perceived as being too bossy?

Oftentimes women will respond that they would rather work for a man than a woman. Why is this? Do young girls give into male authority? Do women support other women with authority? Are women more likely to gossip and spread ill will? If so, is this a learned or innate behavior? If so, why do they think this is professional behavior?

Have you ever observed a woman who appears to support other women, yet all of a sudden, one may feel that another has stabbed them in the back? Some women seem to have a knack at stirring up drama. This regularly occurs in the workplace. Men can disagree with one another by expressing this with some words and get over it. Whereas women are often viewed as stirring the pot by saying things behind someone's back. They never confront the issue directly with the person involved in the matter, yet they are comfortable discussing the problem with others.

Women frequently say that the workplace experience with other women reminded them of high-school drama. The same negative attitudes in the workplace make one question certain mindsets, attitudes, and behaviors of women. Informal observation in the workplace would dictate that more attractive women have less support from the majority of women. This was often observed through personal experience. For some reason, women would often criticize another boss and make it sound like it is for the "good of the organization." Personally, if someone isn't willing to confront the conflict face-to-face or even with another person acting as a neutral listener, then it isn't a problem that needs to be addressed. This is just demeaning another person. This type of aggressive behavior is a way of dealing with competition, conflict, or even seeking attention from the males. This may sound cruel, but it is an elephant in the room that needs to be addressed in the workplace. If this type of behavior is observed, it is necessary to define it, address the situation, and create an action plan for future conflict. This type of behavior should *never* be ignored.

Research states that there is something called "queen bee syndrome." According to Wikipedia, "queen bee syndrome" was first defined by G. L. Staines, T. E. Jayaratne, and C. Tavris in 1973. It describes a woman in a position of authority who views or treats subordinates more critically if they are female. This phenomenon has been documented by several studies. In another study, scientists from the University of Toronto speculated that the queen bee syndrome might be the reason that women find it more stressful to work for women managers; no difference was found in stress levels for male workers. An alternate, though closely related, definition describes a queen bee as one who has succeeded in her career, but refuses to do the same.

This research indicates that this syndrome begins in some girls in middle school and high school when they first experience severe bullying. This inappropriate behavior is usually carried out by one individual who is seen as the leader or queen bee. This person holds such power that for the right or wrong cause, other females will follow.

If this is the case, is it time for a double dose of teaching the importance of kindness to young girls? These inappropriate behaviors are unacceptable and should be immediately addressed when observed. Programs need to ensure that girls are supported as much as boys. It is important to model and teach young girls to voice their strengths and desires to achieve and accomplish great things, while not tearing others down or allowing others' negative words to impact the outcome. Girls need to be reassured that they are powerful and have the ability and courage to take risks, while supporting others who are doing the same.

In the book *The Help*, one of the caregivers would constantly tell the little girl she was raising that she was kind, beautiful, and smart. Do children hear these words enough? Shouldn't we be empowering kids with kind words that build their confidence? It is believed that this positive emotional connection would lead to less bullying and fewer "queen bee syndrome" behaviors.

Do we use such kind words in the workplace? Oftentimes women who achieve high power are often seen as the queen bees. It is even perceived that their behavior and leadership style take on similar traits as their male counterparts as a way to be seen as "one of the boys" or someone with more masculine qualities. This will often legitimize their work, or role, and keep other professionals away to maintain this power.

If women want to change the culture, then they must understand how they are perceived. This will assist with defining a solution, not becoming part of the problem. Think about when you were a young child or student. Didn't you love it when your parents or teachers complimented you for something you did well? People of all ages want to experience success.

Direct feedback is certainly important in the development of skills. People need to be praised when their work behavior and positive attitude exhibited is on target or exceeds the expectation. When the results don't meet expectations, it is also important to provide individual feedback with possible solutions and/or additional training. Everyone wants to experience success and contribute to a high performing team.

There is a first grade teacher named Ashley Keene in Perry Local School District (Perry, OH). She is doing a terrific job recognizing the need to support girls' self-esteem. In this work, she developed a "Mighty Girls" group. The intent is to train girls at a young age how to love and respect themselves and others. The girls created the following goals to support their work:

1. Mighty Girls love themselves and others.
2. Mighty Girls use kind words.
3. Mighty Girls have positive thoughts.
4. Mighty Girls help others.
5. Mighty Girls take care of their bodies.
6. Mighty Girls stand up for themselves and others.

Wouldn't the world be a better place if everyone embraced the same rules? Kudos to Perry Local School District and others that achieve the goal of empowering young children to be the best they can be! What a great way to teach girls to love themselves and support one another. This is an extremely important message.

During some of the seminars on this topic, many female colleagues were interviewed, it was learned that they were taught to be kind and quiet. Girls were to sit pretty and not to voice strong opinions.

One person reported that her father was so upset and quit talking to her when she qualified for the honor roll one semester and not the next. She shared how she never got over that feeling of his disappointment. However, when she was later voted as homecoming queen, her father was very proud of her again. She reported that her self-esteem was certainly impacted by her father's perception of her. What does this inconsistent message send young girls in these transformative years?

Bullying behavior is bred from a lack of confidence. It is important to model effective strategies to children (no matter the gender) so that all understand that they are worthwhile, valued, and that they are supported no matter what the occasion may be.

Children need to be assured that their parents and other adults in their life will always be there for them. It is important that children feel loved for the good, bad, and ugly. If we provide a strong support system for children, they may develop a positive self-esteem. Bullying behaviors eliminate others' confidence. Therefore, they thrive on knocking others down.

In summary, bullying, criticizing, and isolating individuals should never be accepted. It is time to stand up and support one another. Such positive behavior would go a long way in the workplace. As the leader of an organization, it is important to take the sting out of the queen bees. This means that candid conversations need to occur, expectations must be followed, and employees receive direct instruction, feedback, and training. This includes the leader setting the tone and modeling expectations for behavior and attitudes, which shape the mindsets of the organization.

Change occurs from within first and soon it will become contagious for others. Let's work together to model, teach, and change how women leaders are viewed in the workplace.

## PROBLEM-SOLVING SCENARIO

You are in the workroom and overhear a coworker talking negatively about another coworker. They try to pull you into the conversation by asking you to share negative experiences about the employee.

### Questions

1. How do you reply?
2. How can you reply in a positive manner while modeling the importance of supporting one another in the workplace?

### Reflections

- Would you rather work for a man or woman? Why?
- Have you observed bullying in the workplace?

- Do you support your fellow coworkers? How?
- Do you want others to support you?
- What behavior commands respect from others in the workplace?

# PART II

# Successful Female Leaders Understand Where They Are

## Chapter 4

# Changing the Paradigm

Real change, enduring change, happens one step at a time.—Ruth Bader Ginsburg

*A Personal Wish*

*Shifting to a new paradigm is not about adding more stuff. It is about changing mindsets, attitudes, and behaviors. If we want to change the paradigm to increase the number of women bosses, we need to change our way of thinking.*

*This would take major steps toward understanding implicit bias about gender differences and creating a plan of action to address these biases and barriers. It will take a new way of thinking to create an evolution in using our own experiences, research, and tools to approach ways to adapt to new practices. This will take a shift in priority, relationships, purpose, flexibility, and planning.*

*As a mother and grandmother, I hope that these changes happen quickly. I would never want to tell my daughters or granddaughters that they can't achieve their dreams. Isn't it time to make necessary changes in equality?*

The song "Man in the Mirror" by Michael Jackson has some great lyrics about the importance of change and how it starts with each individual (me). Rather than complain about the status quo, wouldn't it be nice if everyone took action for their own personal growth, supported others in their journey, and worked to create a better place for the young females following behind?

In the book *The Confidence Code*, the author talks about how thoughts plus confidence equal action. Now is the time to begin with personal growth and create a plan of action that will create a momentum of change. Where do we want to be in the next five or ten years with gender equality? It is time to begin this movement. Who is ready to begin this momentum? It takes one person to believe they can make the necessary change, to set the expectations for others to follow. It is time to stand up and close the gender disparity gap within all professions. It is time for women to voice the need for change, keeping the emotion positive, while sharing stories that will lead to change.

Parents, teachers, friends, it is time to change the language used with young girls. It is important that children are empowered to achieve their goals and aspirations. Young girls need to feel encouraged to take risks while celebrating the triumphs and failures. Both are opportunities for learning and growth. After all, perseverance will ultimately lead to inner strength.

It is time for young girls and grown women to be encouraged to use their voice and communicate expectations. Women, girls aren't being bossy, they are being strong confident people. Young girls need to be guided to surround themselves with positive role models and understand that there is no such thing as perfect. Girls need to be taught to be kind, caring, honest, and strong. It's time to celebrate imperfections, gain confidence through our experiences, which include mistakes, and create a growth mindset for strength, confidence, and ability to empower others.

It is time for individuals and organizations to share stories and expect active listening to occur between employees. It is no longer acceptable for men or women to talk over one another. When inappropriate behavior or attitude occurs, it shouldn't be ignored. Give yourself permission to use ground rules, norms, and candor to address the situation. This can be done in a very positive and professional manner.

For women in the workplace, it is time to celebrate the skill sets that each individual brings to the table, build one another up, compliment one another's strengths, and empower other female employees to seek opportunities for advancement. All employees thrive by the process of collaboration. This can't be done to the truest potential if people are putting one another down. There are plenty of jobs for everyone working to their maximum potential.

As female mentors, it is our job to look at our organization and pull females forward. It is our obligation to teach, build, and support others so they can advance in the workplace. These strategies will help sustain quality organizations as productivity increases.

Leaders in the top executive positions can begin closing the gender disparity gaps by doing the following:

1. Admitting that gender disparity still exists.
2. Reevaluating policies, procedures, and practices for gender bias on a regular basis.
3. Changing the hiring practice. Are the interview instruments free from bias? Are those making hiring decisions regularly trained to address the focus and beliefs of the organization?
4. Employing training and employee development. Is regular training offered to provide diverse learning experiences for employees?
5. Assessing evaluation instruments. Are they aligned with the organization's vision, mission, values, beliefs, and employee expectations? Are evaluations completed on a regular cycle with appropriate details for strengths and improvement noted?
6. Implementing a compensation plan. Is the compensation plan noted on an approved document, providing levels of experience and bonus compensation plans, ensuring that men and women are paid equal salary for equal work?
7. Do company procedures address life-balance issues? For example, if child care is an issue, does the company institute child care options, policies, etc.?

If organizations truly want to address gender disparity issues, it is time to make the necessary changes for improvement and the removal of barriers.

In summary, it is time to change the paradigm. It begins with each individual, which will create a momentum within others. Now is the time for women to stand together and address the elephant in the room. Women can no longer ignore inappropriate behavior. This only perpetuates the problem. Rather than complain and expect everyone else to change, it is each individual's responsibility to speak up and model the expected behavior. This is what will change attitude, behavior, mindsets, and paradigms. How will you contribute to the necessary change?

Let's challenge one another to look in the mirror, start the change process, and join one another to transform the paradigm for all women.

## PROBLEM-SOLVING SCENARIO

Have you ever met anyone who has changed the way you think about something? A beautiful sixteen-year-old girl, sedulous in nature, attended a student leadership summit where she shared her story about poverty, racism, sexual assault, importance of voice, and survivorship. Being a white, middle aged, and average socioeconomic woman, her story tugged at the heart.

Being from a third-world country, this young lady was the first in her family to receive a formal education. She shared that at age eight, she couldn't wait to go to school. That excitement soon changed once a male leader in the school began raping her. She shared that she spoke up, but things didn't change during her education.

Being a person born of privilege, listening to this story was horrifying. How can this behavior be allowed? It was sad to hear but extremely enlightening to learn how someone overcame such a nightmare and now travels the world sharing the importance of active listening—without judgment and while understanding and taking risks in using their own voice to shape change, using personal struggles and experiences to make change. I truly admire this young lady for using her voice to change my personal thoughts about poverty.

### Questions

1. Have you ever met someone who changed your thinking on a topic?
2. Did this change your attitude, behavior, and mindset? If so, how?

### Reflections

- Do you remember a time when you felt ignored? Explain.
- Do you remember a time when you felt empowered? Explain.
- How do you build personal confidence?
- How do you build the self-esteem of others around you?

- How do you encourage others to voice their feelings and provide input?

*Chapter 5*

# Gender Differences in the Workplace

Every great dream begins with a dreamer. Always remember that you have within you the strength, the patience, and the passion to reach for the stars to change the world.—Harriet Tubman

*Personal Story of Women and Men Bosses*

*The movie The Devil Wears* Prada *is a perfect example of why multiple surveys indicate that women prefer male bosses. Many of my colleagues have said that women are too emotional; don't mentor well; aren't honest about their intentions, giving a fake smile when they really feel differently; are too competitive; are concerned about the dress code more than men; are caring by nature and have difficulty providing constructive feedback; are difficult to please; and have unreasonably high expectations. Many females who have held top leadership positions would strongly disagree with these concerns. Some may even say the statements are examples of implicit biases.—Anonymous author*

## DIFFERENCES IN LEADERSHIP STYLE BETWEEN GENDERS

Effective leaders learn early in their careers to surround themselves with the best people, those who exhibit the following characteristics: trustworthy; good listening skills; good problem-solving skills and the ability to solve problems through consensus building; promote and encourage risk-taking; have high expectations; understand the

31

importance of job and family; and understand the importance of collaboration and team-building, which is part of building a healthy work culture.

In every organization there are people who build others up and people who tear others down. Those that thrive on the misfortune of others tend to call names or cast blame. When such threatening behaviors are allowed to occur, it results in a loss of voice and a toxic work environment. This inappropriate behavior results in a decrease in performance. Statistics prove that people become disconnected and are more likely to leave. Such organizations won't grow and will have a constant turnover.

According to Davis, Capobianco, and Kraus, "Women were rated as significantly more likely to engage in almost every constructive behavior, where men were rated as more likely to engage in active destructive behaviors." Moreover, "Female bosses made more positive ratings of targets than male bosses. In general, bosses rated targets somewhat higher on passive responses."[1]

Behavior differences occur among all genders, races, and creeds; however, it is believed that male and female genetics are different enough that the motivation and drive behind the work can appear different, depending on the situation.

Research on brain development suggests that men are more linear thinkers, while women think in patterns. For example, women see connections like one would find in a Venn diagram. The difference in thinking and reflecting may be a direct cause of some of the characteristics found among many women and men. See table 5.1 for an example.

**Table 5.1. How Women Think Versus How Men Think**

| *Women are more likely to:* | *Men are more likely to:* |
| --- | --- |
| Emphasize relationships and collaboration | Emphasize organizational matters |
| Focus on instructional leadership | Focus on tasks |
| Work to build consensus/support collaboration | Go for majority rules and focus on the win |
| Emphasize the process | Emphasize the product |
| Emphasize feelings of self-worth | Emphasize feelings of accomplishment |
| Engage others and share power and information | Focus on top-down decision making and hoard information |

| Promote the self-interests of others as part of the overall goal | Promote own self-interests as part of the overall goal |
| --- | --- |

According to the Pew Research Center, women are seen as more honest, intelligent, compassionate, outgoing, and creative. Men are seen as more decisive.[2] The important concept is to understand situational leadership. Although women tend to tell stories or make associations with similar experiences and appear to be less direct, it is imperative for women to understand when this style of speaking is appropriate and when it isn't. When in a boardroom, it is important to be decisive and direct, playing the storytelling down. Yet, when leadership meetings and relationship building are necessary, storytelling is a style that works. When in a CEO position, women have to learn when to tone down the female strategies and turn up the male strategies.

In many different studies, it has been reported that people mostly want to work for men. It wasn't until 2017 that Gallup reported a change in these statistics. Today, 55% of men and women reported that they have *no preference. Within this percentage, more men are more likely not* to have a preference. Women under fifty tend to prefer women bosses. The tide appears to be turning. Is this due to different leadership styles or growth mindsets?

In a previous chapter, it was reported that studies report that men tend to sponsor or promote other men better than women sponsor or promote other women. This causes much reflection. Is this an innate characteristic that is birthed out of a competitive nature? Do women compete at a different level than men? Research shared throughout the book indicates that these are certainly learned behaviors.

As a leader, the takeaway from such studies is to create a plan that identifies ways to support, sponsor, and mentor those demonstrating potential for future leadership work. Be the mentor and sponsor that you wish you had. Women should *always* demonstrate their strengths, not downplay them. They should quit making their ideas look like someone else's idea. They should start accepting compliments by saying thank you instead of changing the topic or making excuses for the positive skill set. Women need to support one another and learn from one another so that they become the *best* they can be. Every leader needs to lead with care and understanding for themselves and others.

Women can learn from one another by displaying awareness and acceptance, complimenting others for their work capabilities, mentoring, and providing opportunities for people to learn and meet other top-ranking executives with hiring power.

Women, by nature, have the ability to nurture. Let's be more conscientious about the importance of implementing relationship builder strategies that we know lead to effective work environments and improved performance. Relationship builders understand the importance of the following leadership strategies:

1. Investing in people
2. Displaying a positive attitude
3. Being real—telling stories of triumph and tragedy
4. Encouraging reflective practice and being good communicators
5. Implementing problem-solving strategies
6. Displaying a willingness to serve others
7. Providing feedback on and an appreciation of work

These strategies are very similar to those outlined in an article in the *Harvard Business Review*, which indicates that there are five characteristics of leaders that people want to follow: ability to empower others, active listening skills, motivation to delegate work and build trust, willingness to take ownership and responsibility, and consistency.[3] Again, relationships make a difference.

In summary, it is important to understand that generally speaking, male and female executives are wired differently. How one communicates, collaborates, and interacts with others can appear competitive in nature. Women shouldn't personalize these differences or see it as a threat. It is important to understand the different styles and use the attributes to communicate and interact accordingly.

## PROBLEM-SOLVING SCENARIO

You are a female superintendent who works with a male treasurer. You are in a public board meeting and learn of a new facility project for the first time. This information was a discussion under new business but wasn't listed in detail on the agenda. It is obvious that the board received new information that you (as the superintendent) were *not* privy to.

## Questions

1. How do you address the communication problem?
2. What do you do if the problem continues?
3. Would this happen if two males were working in these power positions? Why? Why not?

## Reflections

- What leadership characteristics do you admire?
- Do you have professional or personal friends who are different from you in race, gender, socioeconomic status, etc.?
- Do you personalize differences?
- How do you want to be viewed as a leader?

## NOTES

1. Mark H. Davis, Sal Capobianco, & Linda A. Kraus. (2010). "Gender Differences in Responding to Conflict in the Workplace: Evidence Found in a Large Sample of Working Adults." *Sex Roles 63*, no. 7: 500.

2. "Men or Women: Who's the Better Leader?" Pew Research Center, August 25, 2008, https://www.pewresearch.org/social-trends/2008/08/25/men-or-women-whos-the-better-leader/.

3. Sunnie Giles, "The Most Important Leadership Competencies, According to Leaders Around the World." *Harvard Business Review*, March 15, 2016, https://hbr.org/2016/03/the-most-important-leadership-competencies-according-to-leaders-around-the-world.

## Chapter 6

# Attitudes, Behaviors, and Mindsets

I would rather regret the things that I've done than the things I haven't done.—Lucille Ball

*Personal Story of Attitudes/Behaviors/Mindsets*

*You could describe this famous fable* The Tortoise and the Hare *as a battle of fixed versus growth mindsets. Instead of believing, "I'm too slow to race," the tortoise boldly takes the challenge. The tortoise demonstrates the growth mindset and challenges himself to move forward. On the other hand, the hare demonstrates the fixed mindset with his arrogance and confidence that nothing will stop him from winning the race. This story represents how anyone can change their trajectory by focusing on the goal and making small changes for improvement. You can do this!*

What occurs in early stages of life that impacts the differences in attitudes, behaviors, and mindsets between genders? By reflecting upon your early school experiences, often one would observe young boys playing team sports, while young girls role-play different things on the playground. There is definitely a difference in team play versus relationship play. Research indicates that there is learned behavior among different genders. One would think this contributes to differences observed within the workplace.

Dr. Pat Heim, CEO and author, states, "In the workplace there are fundamental and biological differences." She goes as far as saying, "Men and women live in different worlds as it pertains to introducing ideas, receiving criticism, and not knowing the answer."[1] Her research reports differences in the following behaviors:

1. Hierarchy versus relationships
2. Goals versus process
3. Authority versus engagement
4. Team play versus team players
5. Attribution of success

This research is eye-opening. It creates much reflection about the differences in communication and problem solving in the workplace. In the book *Men Are from Mars and Women Are from Venus*, author John Gray states that there are definite differences between the way the different genders communicate.[2] Similar to this idea, Heim's research shows that women see things in circles, while men see things in linear form. Women are relationship-builders and see everyone at the table as having an equal voice. When it comes to goals, both are focused on outcomes, but how they are achieved differ. Women are focused on the process, which includes collaboration, while men are focused on just the outcome; the process isn't as important.

Personal experience indicates that women are more likely to seek input from others when problem solving. Women are good at demonstrating resilience and reflection. Women leaders are known to support their team by creating safe places for open reflection and collaboration. Stories about failure are seen as important as those about successes.

Unless company training and/or common practice dictates differently, men oftentimes sort through the options alone before coming up with a solution. Men get directly to the point and don't appear to appreciate the value in storytelling. At times, women are viewed as weak when their communication style isn't direct, making them appear indecisive.

Another difference is how men and women see success. When women succeed, they often contribute this success to others. They rarely take the credit. When most men experience success, they own their own skills that contributed to the success. Why do women downplay their skills or make their ideas appear to be someone else's? As a woman, it is believed that this is learned behavior because they don't want to be a target of other women. Typically, women don't support other women in the workplace like men do. How do we begin to change this mindset within individuals and the paradigm within each organization?

As a former superintendent, there were times when men and women in executive positions would disagree. During conflict, men appeared more direct with their word choice, while women tend to be less direct and ask questions. Women frequently view men as territorial and even bullies, while women are viewed as soft or passive aggressive. Understanding such differences is power. This understanding and knowledge will set you free from fear and assist in perfecting your personal strengths. Understanding the differences will allow better collaboration and improved communication and outcomes.

Research shows that gender roles are a learned behavior and are not innate. The *Sage Encyclopedia of Psychology and Gender* states,

> Gender development refers to the process by which individuals construct their internal sense of self within the context of societal gender norms. Gender norms include traits stereotypically associated with genetic males ("masculine traits," e.g., aggression, dominance, and competitiveness) and those associated with genetic females ("feminine traits," e.g., nurturance, innocence, and passivity).[3]

This definition gives hope that mindsets, attitudes, and behavior can be changed.

Teachers have the opportunity on a daily basis to observe different genders, personalities, and interests. They will soon learn the importance of how the environment impacts individual development. Statements like "Boys will be boys and girls will be girls" reinforce stereotypes. If young children stop hearing reinforcement on stereotypes and begin hearing more words that reinforce positive behavior, mindsets and attitude would change. Children need to be consistently taught confidence and to like themselves and others. They will also learn a common language to navigate such differences. These characteristics go a long way in opening the hearts and minds to value differences. Wouldn't this be a terrific start in the changing of the paradigm toward gender disparity.

If organizations implemented consistent practices that contribute to a positive and healthy culture, things would improve. It is *never* too late to begin this process. Let's stand together to build others up and support one another. Be positive, not negative. Now more than ever it is important to love one another, show compassion and understanding, and support one another's gifts. There is room for everyone to share their gifts.

## PROBLEM-SOLVING SCENARIO

You are one of two executive directors in an organization. You are the only female executive director and are in charge of curriculum. The male executive director is in charge of personnel. As part of your training, you must both deliver information to new employees. Your agenda includes using a game to deliver the key points. His part of the agenda is a "sit-and-get" delivery method. During the meeting and in front of the new employees, the male director throws off on the "hands-on-delivery" method of delivery and eludes that he doesn't have time for games. The new employees look directly to you and the other director to see what is going to happen next.

## Questions

1. What just happened? Why?
2. How do you handle it?
3. What do you do if this becomes the status quo for future interactions?

## Reflections

- What characteristics do you look for in a leader?
- What leadership qualities motivate you to improve your results?
- Do you feel that personal mindsets, behaviors, and attitude persuade your thinking about leadership style?
- What is your personal takeaway from this chapter?

## NOTES

1. Pat Heim. (2015). *Hardball for Women: Winning at the Game of Business.* New York: Plume, 67.

2. John Gray. (2012). *Men Are from Mars and Women Are from Venus*. New York: Harper Paperbacks.

3. Chassitty N. Whitman & Theresa Fiani. "Behavioral Theories of Gender Development." *Sage Encyclopedia of Psychology and Gender*, https:// sk.sagepub.com/reference/the-sage-encyclopedia-of-psychology-and-gender/ i2642.xml.

# PART III

# Successful Female Leaders Understand the Importance of a Healthy Culture

# Chapter 7

# Relationships Matter

Treat your friends as you do your best pictures and place them in their best light.—Lady Randolph Churchill, 1854–1921

*Relationships Really Do Matter!*

*The following poem represents a personal experience of some educators who met on an educational trip to Finland and have been friends ever since. A necklace was purchased with the following poem to represent their friendship:*

*Sometimes in life the* right *people come into your life and never leave. They are the people that celebrate on your brightest days but also comfort you on the darkest nights. They are the* light bringers *and the* dream boosters. *They* elevate, challenge, *and* believe in *you. They remind you that every night has a day and every scar can be healed. You may not see one another often as you'd like, but when you catch up, it* lights up the whole sky. *These people are more than just your friends—they are your* squad. *Hold onto them, love them, and protect them.* You're truly better together!—*Bryan Anthony*

Relationships are at the center of everything we do. May it be with family, friends, or coworkers, relationships matter. Positive work relationships fuel self-discovery and self-actualization. The more we are engaged and present in the moment, the more people benefit.

The research is clear that humans are wired with the desire to connect. We are beings that thrive on healthy relationships. Yet, in our schools and in the workplace the importance of building and sustaining positive relationships can be overlooked. According to training received through

Gallup Poll, relationships are the most important instructional strategy in the classroom. It was also learned that 70% of employee engagement is based on relationships. In the summer of 2021, Gallup reported that 48% of U.S. employees are actively searching for job opportunities. Gallup found that disengaged workers are at the highest risk of leaving. It takes a pay raise of more than 20% to lure most employees away from a manager who engages them. High-quality managers who inspire and support their teams are an effective mode of protection for retaining their most talented workers.[1]

If relationships are so important to a person's well-being and productivity at work, why isn't this a part of company training, expectations, and mission statements? It is surprising how little company training is devoted to such an important attribute of a quality organization.

Despite the proven connection between positive relationships and success, some people dismiss the importance of this skill and expectation. If you are interested in building positive relationships, it is important to implement the following strategies:

1. Communicate expectations and set boundaries in a way that others respect and want to follow.
2. Recognize individual talents and skill sets.
3. Create a community where diversity is respected and individuality is embraced.
4. Share personal interests and values.
5. Learn the names of and something personal about your direct reports.
6. Examine and improve verbal and nonverbal communication. Employees need to understand expectations and how they fit into the overall strategic plan. Nonverbal communication can be easily misunderstood. If there is a conflict between the verbal and nonverbal communication, it interferes with the ability to trust a supervisor.
7. Treat everyone with dignity and respect, and without judgment.

These strategies will build positive relationships and trust in an organization.

When people are in the moment and truly engaged with one another, there are increased opportunities to develop and cultivate relationships.

At work, it is important for employees to know that they are cared for and valued. This can be done by remembering family members' names and asking them how individual family members are doing. It can be as simple as checking in with a coworker when they return from vacation and seeing if they enjoyed their time away from the office. Coworkers certainly have time for such informal conversations around the workroom, water fountain, or coffeepot. Seize the moment.

When positive relationships are established, it is easier to have candid conversations within the workplace. This will challenge personal growth and push individuals to improve through their personal and professional talents and skill sets. This is another way to build trust and relationships.

It is also important to provide support when someone takes a risk and the outcome isn't what was expected. Another way to provide support is to assist others in completing their tasks or assigned goals. After all, if we're truly being a servant leader and sharing leadership with others, these are great strategies to assist others in their development.

Collaboration is a great way to develop relationships. Organizations that implement ground rules, communicate a clear sense of purpose, and define roles will increase their performance. Sharing power will build the team and enhance opportunity for growth. It is important to connect employees with the right people and in the right place and time. Again, seize the moments.

In summary, relationships are imperative to one's personal and professional growth. Connections need to be made before compliance becomes a consistent way of operation. Employees tend to thrive in environments where people feel valued and respected, and have the opportunity to engage in problem solving. With the right relationships, anything can be accomplished. Trust, respect, communication, all contribute to the relationships established. With this, goals will be defined, habits will be established, and positive change will occur.

## PROBLEM-SOLVING SCENARIO

You are a new principal assigned to a middle school in a rural area. A big part of the job assignment is to deal with student discipline. You were investigating a fight between two boys in the restroom. After the investigation, both boys are suspended for two days outside of school. As you call the parents to inform them of the incident and due process, one of the fathers asks to speak to the male principal, thinking that a woman doesn't understand the issue—that boys will fight.

## Questions

1. How do you respond? Why?

## Reflections

- What relationships in your life do you value the most? Why?
- What relationships in your life would you like to improve? Why?
- How can you begin making better connections and building trust with this person or others?

### NOTE

1. Ryan Pendell, "7 Workplace Insights: What We Learned in 2021," Gallup Workplace, January 21, 2022, https://www.gallup.com/workplace/358346/gallup-workplace-insights-learned-2021.aspx#:~:text=In%20the%20summer%20of%202021,and%20rethink%20their%20employer%20brand.

## Chapter 8

# The Importance of Creating
# a Healthy Culture

Real integrity is doing the right thing, knowing that no one will ever know you did it.—Oprah Winfrey

*Culture-Building During a Pandemic*

*Much like people who remember where they were when John F. Kennedy was shot in 1963 or when the space shuttle* Challenger *crashed in 1986, a memory imprinted in my mind is when Ohio governor Mike DeWine and Dr. Amy Acton mandated a state closure of schools in 2020. As a school district chief officer for student instruction, rather than panic, I saw an opportunity to experience something profound and ignite culture among our PreK–12 staff. This would be an experience where we would rise from a global pandemic together and be forever changed—for the better. The opportunity: win the moment.*

*When a teaching organization pivots 180 degrees to move instruction and student well-being from in person to virtual classrooms, a leader has the choice (and opportunity) to intentionally plan for the experience our actions will deliver to our parents, students, and staff. We can panic or perform. Our team quickly senses the leadership style we have ignited. With a culture rooted in trust and results, it's clear to see character, connections, clarity, support, and accountability. In school cultures like this, the team has the foundation to withstand even a global pandemic. What did this look like for a healthy school culture in March 2020?*

*Clarity: Provide clear yet attainable guidance.*

> *Support: Don't ask your team to do anything you aren't willing to do.*
> *Plan chunks of essential training with practice time.*
> *Character: This means saying what you mean and consistently doing*
> *what you say. Be vulnerable in showing that you too are humble*
> *and growing each day. This ship stays on course no matter how*
> *high the waters rise.*
> *Connections: Infuse joy and laughter in our precious moments with*
> *staff. Give individuals space to fail, laugh, or cry together, and*
> *try again with guidance and grace—whatever it takes.* Everyone
> matters.

*Intentional leadership navigates each moment, each day, each month. When we lose a moment, be sure to win the next two.[1] Watch the ways in which we engage in meetings through culture. Watch the ways in which we show up for one another and our families, even parading to the homes of each child. Watch the ways we check in with our mates and give anyone on any day a moment to "tap out," and we cover their work because we care. Watch our school teams rise from the ashes of strife in the most beautiful example of the human spirit—culture.—Dr. Betty Jo Malchesky*

In 2021, the *New York Times* reported that for women, hostility is out in the open toward other women at one professional conference. Data from the National Bureau of Economic Research supports this. At this conference, women are less likely to be chosen to speak, are more likely to encounter greater barriers in getting published, and receive 12% more questions than men. Some women reported that they avoid speaking at the conference because they fear disrespectful treatment.[2] This is just another example of gender bias.

It is time to expect more change with gender bias issues and not be passive when we see others resist the need to do the right thing. Those that resist change try to marginalize others and attack and promote fear through name calling, blame, or killing the messenger tactics. When this occurs, it is necessary to create a system that institutionalizes healthy habits for positive working conditions.

Change can be uncomfortable when it challenges values, beliefs, and behaviors that have occurred for long periods of time. It requires loss, uncertainty, and sometimes a feeling of disloyalty to those that promote a negative work culture. Some discomfort is necessary, but too much can lead to immobility.

It is important that organizations think about ways to create healthy work cultures that support women with family obligations, change the perception of the "old boys club," and create training and mentor programs that prepare *everyone* for job advancement.

Promoting positive relationships contributes to a healthy, productive workplace culture. A workplace culture is the shared values, belief systems, and attitudes, and assumptions people share and practice. Research indicates that a positive culture improves teamwork, raises morale, increases efficiency and productivity, and enhances retention in the workplace. Organizations that establish a healthy culture create ambitious goals and visions. They intentionally shape and support the culture by implementing protocols and norms. These systems create opportunity for consensus building, engagement, and buy in.

Does this describe an environment that you would like to be a part of? Healthy work environments tend to be more collaborative, where people share the importance of the overall result and understand their role in achieving this work. It is one that encourages problem solving as a team. Through this practice norms are institutionalized such as active listening and valuing the strengths of each teammate. This builds trust and engages employees to commit to the goal and end product.

Toxic workplaces tend to make top-down decisions and blame others for the lack of results. There is no room for "queen bees" or anyone who intimidates others or promotes fear in an organization. Where such behaviors are modeled, one will find a lack of trust, less engagement, and lower performance outcomes. It just takes one leader to demonstrate or allow such inappropriate behavior, which sets the tone for the entire organization. When this occurs, the culture becomes toxic and no one benefits.

Leaders need to set high expectations, communicate a clear message, consistently model the expected outcomes, and empower employees to work with their personal strengths and skill sets. Sharing leadership with those that demonstrate strengths and an ability to lead is a great way to mentor. Individuals that are placed in such roles claim that this practice is rewarding and builds trust within the team. This should be a consistent practice for all leaders within an organization.

If an unhealthy organization is inherited, it is important to take a step back and analyze the needs while setting the expectation. Often this will involve some homework on the leader's part to use historical data to determine the root cause to the toxic culture. To build capacity, it will involve sharing the data as to why the change in behavior is imperative to increase productivity, performance, and overall results.

As a former elementary school principal, it was discovered during the first year of a new assignment that there was a discipline issue. There was no time to conduct building walk-throughs because of the number of student discipline referrals each day. The referrals would be for minor infractions such as forgetting homework to severe infractions such as bullying or fighting. When the staff studied the data, they decided that the minor infractions would best be addressed through the teacher. A new strategy of implementing an after-school detention process was implemented as part of the classroom discipline.

The severe referrals for inappropriate behavior would still result in an office visit, parent conference, as a minimum outcome. Depending on the type of infraction, it could also result in a more severe outcome. This minor change in the building discipline process empowered the staff.

The staff reported that they appreciated having input to the building discipline, and the process of the decision making made them feel valued. Therefore, the additional time put forth in the process was well invested. This collaboration produced a building plan that led to systematic changes, which increased learning. The building became a School of Promise within a year.

This is a good example of how data was used to problem solve and how a collaborative effort led to improved outcomes for the adults and learners. With a focused action plan, strategies, and measurements, growth will occur.

Building awareness leads to understanding. Once people begin understanding the need for change, ownership begins to occur. With consistency, capacity will build quickly. If we want to make change with gender bias in the workplace, it is important to use not only the strategies found in a healthy workplace, but also voice and choice to build awareness.

A great resource for work on disparity issues is a tool called the "Proficiency Continuum," found in the book *Cultural Proficiency: A Manual for School Leaders*. The authors use a conceptual framework of cultural proficient practices. When analyzing differing worldviews an unhealthy practice would involve the following strategies:

Cultural destructiveness: Using one's power to eliminate the culture of another.

Cultural incapacity: Believing in the superiority of one's own culture and behaving in ways that disempowered another's culture.

Cultural blindness: Acting as if cultural differences do not matter.

When analyzing differing worldviews, one that depicts a healthy practice includes the following strategies:

Cultural precompetence: Recognizing the limitations of one's skills or an organization's practices.

Cultural competence: Interacting with others using the essential elements of understanding: valuing diversity, managing the dynamics of differences, adapting to diversity, and institutionalizing cultural knowledge.

Cultural proficiency: Interacting and engaging with other cultures.[3]

This tool provides a framework to engage organizations in dialogue about where they stand within certain contexts and with certain practices. If considering gender bias, which competency does your organization practice? It is imperative to allow multiple perspectives to be shared through personal stories. This provides perspective and an understanding of where the organization wants to be. If an organization recognizes limitations but there isn't a framework to structure the work, it will be difficult to move forward with a change in the culture.

How do we begin to address barriers? Let's start by celebrating the attitudes, beliefs, and values that support gender equality. Let's also begin by women understanding their skill sets and strengths, and not hesitating to promote them appropriately. Celebrating women that display confidence, creativity, kindness, and emotional intelligence is a great way to begin this work.

When considering gender disparity, women need to use their voice and not hesitate to share their personal stories. Men and women need to actively listen, understand the needs, and support differences pertaining to social privileges. This practice will build positive support systems and relationships.

Work environments that are responsible in this movement will display the following characteristics:

1. Become aware and educate others.
2. Create safe workspaces to support those in transition into leadership roles. Eliminate threats by assigning mentors.
3. Focus on women's development efforts by changing policy and procedures for hiring and sustaining quality staff.

Organizations that do this are giving women insight into themselves and their organizations, enabling them to chart a course of action to an advanced position.

It is important that *all* CEOs begin this work by modeling the expectations found within a healthy culture. Consistently implementing expectations and encouraging an environment where feedback and voice are a part of the learning and understanding will help establish an atmosphere that will solve challenges. Collaboration and reflection need to be embedded in the work and aligned to the vision of the organization.

In summary, the culturally proficient organization will have a healthy environment where courageous conversations about equity issues are allowed to occur. Opportunities for people to share personal stories without interruptions, blame, or shame will contribute to improved policies and procedures. This work will eventually become infused with meaning and lead to improved outcomes for all.

As we move forward in improving the gender disparity, many leaders understand the impact of the following quote from an unknown author: *"Don't tell me what you believe, show me what you do, and I'll tell you what you believe."* What a great quote to sum up the meaning of the importance of a healthy work culture. May these words resonate within and drive the work as individuals strive to improve the workplace culture for all employees. It's time to embed these practices in every organization.

## PROBLEM-SOLVING SCENARIO

You are an administrator in a large district. The central office staff calls a planning meeting to improve student performance. After two days of difficult conversations and district agreement, a plan is put into place. Everyone on the team feels good about the ability to collaborate on such an important practice.

You go back to your building and share the new district plan at the building wide staff meeting. The following week, you are called back into the district for another meeting only to learn that the board didn't approve the plan, nor did you realize that it needed board approval since it wasn't policy. You are told to go back to your building and redirect the staff with the board plan, not the administrative plan.

### Questions

1. How did this exercise make you feel?
2. How do you deliver the new plan?
3. What does this activity inform you about the district culture?
4. If you can't support yourself, do you stay?

### Reflections

- Have you ever been engaged or worked in an unhealthy culture? What attributes contributed to the illness found within the environment?
- Have you been engaged or worked in a healthy culture? What attributes created the healthy atmosphere?
- Do you celebrate differences within your environment and/or workplace?
- How do you engage with others unlike you? Do you value differences?

## NOTES

1. T. Kight, keynote address, Perry Local Schools, 2018.

2. Ben Casselman, "For Women in Economics, the Hostility Is Out in the Open." *New York Times*, February 23, 2021, https://www.nytimes.com/2021/02/23/business/economy/economics-women-gender-bias.html

3. Randall B. Lindsey, Kikanza Nuri-Robins, Raymond D. Terrell, & Dolores B. Lindsey. (2018). *Cultural Proficiency: A Manual for School Leaders*, 4th ed. Thousand Oaks, CA: Corwin.

## Chapter 9

# Habits of Successful
# Women Leaders

Only I can change my life. No one can do it for me.—Carol Burnett

*Five Habits of Successful Women*

*Have you read that successful people make their beds every day? I am not sure if successful women fall into that category. We are often too busy taking care of our families and everyone else. But there are some self-care habits of successful women that I have identified unscientifically in my years in education.*

1. *She exercises. She may be the woman that gets up at 5 a.m. to do yoga or the one that walks around her child's soccer practice field in the evening. It is something regular, and although it may be skipped on occasion, it is something she schedules.*
2. *She builds strong relationships with other successful women. This doesn't necessarily mean she goes to lunch weekly with her best friends, but it certainly means that she has people to call to discuss big decisions, cheers on the accomplishments of other women, and takes the time every once in a while to grab a coffee or a cocktail with these colleagues and friends.*
3. *She unplugs. Even if it is for a short period of time each day or each week, there is a time when the phone and the computer are not within arm's reach. She understands that the world will not end if she waits an hour to respond to a phone call, text, or email.*
4. *She has a passion for something outside of work. This is often family, but it can also be a hobby, pets, or volunteering.*

5. *She helps other women and men grow, find their own passions, and grow their leadership skills.—Dr. Nancy L. Wagner*

Have you ever wondered why there are three men to every one woman who is appointed to the top executive roles? Also, if you happen to be the one woman who is appointed to the executive position, what traits and habits do you portray that led to getting this top position?

Few females crack the code to landing the top executive positions. Those that do get the top position have a more diverse background, noting several positions with more years of experience, compared to men. Many have a long-term goal to achieve a leadership position for many years before they actually get the top executive role. Successful female leaders possess the following key qualities: 1) moral grit, 2) drive, 3) problem-solving skills, 4) directness and sometimes assertiveness, 5) innovation, 6) optimism, and 7) the ability to build relationships.

Research indicates that women are typically older before being appointed to such positions, which doesn't contribute to long-term assignments. Another interesting fact is that the few female leaders that get top positions are often appointed to some of the most challenging positions. Their risk-taking, ability to seek expert opinions, grit, ability to manage ambiguity, and ability to empower others are seen as strengths. However, once these organizations go through the necessary change, it is often difficult for them to hang on to the lead position. Often, women in top CEO positions are brought in to be the change agent, which is difficult to survive if boards don't understand the long-term plan; therefore, such planning is necessary at the onset of such appointments. Constant turnover doesn't create long-term results. It would benefit organizations to have a clear plan in place to sustain the top-quality female executives and to carry out the long-term strategic plan.

A mentor has sponsored many women that make it to the CEO position. They are often told they play more like a man. What does this mean? In previous chapters, research indicates that it isn't the *"what"* that makes the difference, it is the *how*, the process, which makes the difference. It is also the understanding between gender differences that will empower individuals to respond accordingly to the situation at hand. In addition, it is the hard work ethic, enthusiasm, and confidence displayed within the female leaders that make others want to follow.

Effective leaders are passionate about the work. This passion drives their ambition, interest in the work, and perseverance to achieve outcomes. They are action oriented and willing to take responsibility. Effective leaders communicate with clarity and are concise with the messaging. They act with a good balance between vision and purpose. Their passion doesn't interfere with their communication. They are good listeners and value self and others.

Successful leaders optimize their performance through the use of their talents, strengths, and skill sets. Effective leaders are also good relationship builders and are found to be approachable and open to differences. These strengths contribute to a healthy culture and increased performance.

Many of the aforementioned attributes of successful female leaders are also found in successful male leaders, as they are traits of high performers. They certainly understand their strengths and weaknesses. Effective leaders focus on their strengths. In the book *Strength Finders 2.0*, Tom Rath suggests that one strategy is to "partner with someone that has more talent in the areas lacking." He also suggests that by knowing your strengths and weaknesses, one can avoid barriers to the weaknesses and gain more strength in the areas identified as natural talent through knowledge and practice.[1]

High performers learn to compensate for their deficits. Creating goals, strategies, and measurements accomplishes this. Most successful people begin implementing goals through small changes within their daily habits. Habits are much easier to start and practice and it leads to bigger results. For example: The goal is to become healthier, the habit is to walk thirty minutes a day. The practice of walking makes the person thirstier and tired. Therefore, they drink more water and sleep longer hours. This habit may lead to the person wanting to eat better. Therefore, the overall outcome leads to improved health.

Let's put this idea into a professional goal. There is a professional want, need, and desire to seek professional advancement. The habit is to attend networking opportunities one time a month. Attending the networking sessions will lead to more contacts, contacts will lead to a better understanding of job opportunities. Now, the applicant has a better idea of vacancies and the employer or designee has a face to associate with the resume.

Another professional goal may be that when conflict occurs or inappropriate behavior is observed, not to ignore. The habit to develop is to start small. Find one opportunity a week that you can use candor to professionally address an inappropriate behavior or attitude that is observed and seen as ineffective. For example, as a female you observe males talking for you in a team meeting. Rather than ignoring and complimenting him for stating what you were thinking, try speaking up by saying, "Excuse me. I thought the question was directed to me" or "Thank you for thinking that you are helping me, but I would like to speak for myself."

Successful women leaders have learned to empower themselves by taking small opportunities to create change. Those in top positions have learned to use candorusing direct but professional words to address inappropriate behavior. Successful women tend to have a knack at building community while addressing needs.

According to James Clear, author of *Atomic Habits*, habits are tiny changes with remarkable results. They should be obvious, easy, attractive, and satisfying. Habits are small steps toward a larger goal. A large goal becomes far more doable when it is broken down into small steps.[2]

As a professional it is important to reflect upon areas that can be improved by developing small habits that lead toward a larger goal. What habits would you like to improve? Often professionals talk about the need to refuel. Such habits may include some of the following: Get good sleep, eat healthy, make time for meditation, exercise, reflect daily upon the work, educate themselves, focus, organize, refine the schedule to find more time, surround themselves with a strong support system, take time to network, take risks, ask for help when needed, and repeat.

The characteristics of male and female leaders are different due to learned behavior. However, effective leaders do portray similar strengths. Due to different demands taking place in personal lives or situational leadership styles, habits may vary between genders. The important message here is to know your strengths, compensate for deficits, and take time for yourself on a personal and professional level to refuel and operate at an optimum level.

In summary, there are certainly similar characteristics found in successful leaders. Those who crack the code to landing the top executive positions have similar qualities. However, due to learned behavior, implementing personal skill sets can appear very different. It is important to directly communicate their long-term goal(s) and be active in seeking a variety of job experiences (including getting a sponsor) and applying for the executive roles of interest.

Once the leadership position is secured, understand the gender differences and use this knowledge to your advantage. Women and men will communicate and process differently. This is understandable and it should never be personalized or seen as weak in nature. Everyone has personal strengths, qualities, and should freely voice them to personally perform at their optimum level.

## PROBLEM-SOLVING SCENARIO

You have been assigned your first leadership role. You are the only female on an all-male leadership team. (What an honor!) At the beginning of each weekly meeting, you are asked to get the men coffee and set up for the meeting.

### Questions

1. How do you view this scenario?
2. Would this be any different if the last person hired was a male?
3. How does this make you feel? How do you handle it?

### Reflections

- What are your strengths? Do you use them to improve your weaknesses?
- During conflict, do you shut down or use your voice to actively participate?
- What new habits would you like to develop? Why?

## NOTES

1. Tom Rath. (2007). *Strength Finders 2.0*. New York: Gallup Press, 23.
2. James Clear. (2018). *Atomic Habits: An Easy and Proven Way to Build Good Habits and Break Bad Ones*. New York: Avery.

# PART IV

# Successful Female Leaders Know Where They Are Headed

# Chapter 10

# The Importance of
# Career Planning

Surround yourself with only the people that will take you higher.—
Oprah Winfrey

*Personal Story About Career Planning*

*The best female mentor I ever had the pleasure of working with is a lady named Adrienne James, former principal of Blue Ash Elementary in Sycamore Community Schools (Ohio). Adrienne later advanced to superintendent of Sycamore Community Schools prior to her retirement. She gave me my first opportunity out of the classroom.*

*I believe that she selected me because we were very opposite in our style. I'm certain she was looking to fill her gaps, as she filled mine. Adrienne was classy and professional. I was "what you see is what you get." Adrienne always took time during and outside of the school day to discuss needs, assign tasks, reflect upon work, and challenge me to improve.*

*One experience was particularly eye-opening. It was my first year out of the classroom where I was expected to give feedback to adults. I was uncomfortable with this since many of the adults were older than me. This was certainly a new experience. I had received a parent complaint about their child's teacher. When conferencing with the teacher I spent the majority of the time discussing all the things I appreciated about the teacher. I'm certain she felt that this conference was about her strengths.*

*Rather than focus on the noted concern at hand, I side tracked the conversation. By the time I got to the complaint, the teacher was feeling so good about herself that she would have been shocked to hear or understand the complaint at hand.*

*I will never forget Adrienne's reaction. She informed me that the experience was like blowing up a big balloon and then popping it. This advice stuck with me for the rest of my career.*

*When giving words for improvement, I always used less words to get to the point before seeking feedback and opening the conversation to questions and examples for growth (if necessary).*

*Thank you, Adrienne. I will always remember the time we worked together and the valuable time you gave me for my own personal reflection and growth. You truly challenged me to be a better professional.—Kelly Murray Spivey*

It is important for those who want to climb the corporate ladder to have a focused career plan. This doesn't just include keeping an active resume on file, this also includes professional development. Successful leaders demonstrate an understanding of different leadership styles, communication styles, the need to mentor/sponsor other potential leaders, investing in professional growth to seek the job of their choice, and the importance of how a healthy work culture cultivates better outcomes.

As individuals think about career advancement opportunities, it is important to have a clear understanding of the position desired, skill sets needed, salary potential, and type of organization preferred to work in. You can make anything happen! You are the navigator of your future.

Begin designing your career map early on. Keep a resume on file and update it annually. Resumes should include skills, evidence of experiences, and improved outcomes aligned with the job description. It is most important to include power words in the resume—empowered, sparked, achieved, stimulated, launched, and so forth. Also, give permission to approach the conversation of job advancement opportunities during evaluation conferences and ask for ways to be mentored and sponsored. Don't fear the question.

It is important to market your work and become indispensable to the organization. Let people know what you desire and how you plan to achieve it. Have you ever heard of dressing for the job you desire, not the one you have? These strategies will lead to advancement.

Multiple reports suggest that women are often high achievers and performers, yet don't apply for upper positions, get passed over for the management positions, or are in similar jobs at a less rate of pay? Is this because women are more likely to communicate differently? Are women more process oriented? If so, does this appear "touchy-feely" and possibly weak? Maybe this is because women aren't mentored or supported the same way as men in the workplace.

Earlier chapters noted that research indicates women and men display different styles within their leadership qualities. Men and women certainly communicate, problem solve, and mentor differently. Women naturally communicate using stories to stress their key points, problem solve through collaboration, and rarely mentor/sponsor another potential leader without being asked.

Knowing there are gender differences with leadership styles, it is important to understand that this is reality and understand when and where certain styles are best played out. Women appear to use more stories to stress a point and are more likely to collaborate when problem solving, while men may view these strategies as a "touchy feely" practice or as time wasted. Although there is research on the benefits of such techniques contributing to a healthy culture, there are certain times when women need to pull back and get directly to the point.

Successful leaders have learned situational leadership strategies. They know when and where to implement their innate or learned skill sets according to the setting. When an executive female is making an important point in the boardroom of males, this isn't the time for enhanced storytelling. During this time, it is important to be direct, make the point, support the point with details, and make the point again. If this isn't a natural skill, it is one that is learned along the way for females desiring top level position.

Reports indicate that men will do more than mentor on the job. They actually sponsor a candidate by socializing outside of work and network with other CEOs with their mentee. Men will network outside of the workplace by playing golf, basketball, going to lunch, dinner, or happy hours. During this informal time, they discuss future opportunities and how they can be promoted. Women are less likely to take another woman under their wing and teach them necessary skill sets, expose others to the inner circles that are responsible for promotion, and promote other women leaders within an organization. Table 10.1 describes the differences between mentors and sponsors.

Women often don't take the time outside of the workplace to attend networking events. Understanding that there are obligations in the

68 *Chapter 10*

**Table 10.1. Differences Between Mentors and Sponsors**

| Mentor | Sponsor |
|---|---|
| Can sit at any level of hierarchy | Must be a senior manager |
| Provides feedback on how to improve | Helps the mentee navigate politics within the organization |
| Serves as a role model | Makes sure their people are considered for challenging assignments |
| Strives to increase the sense of self-worth and competence of mentees | Fights to get their people the job |
| Focuses on mentees' personal and professional development | |
| Protects their protégé from negative publicity | |

home, time isn't always put aside for this important task. Women would greatly benefit from mentoring and sponsoring other women by seeking out talent, making time to point out others' strengths, and setting time aside to assist with career planning.

As an organization striving for optimum performance, it understands the importance of creating a sustainability plan. These plans should include a strong mentorship and sponsorship plans for both genders. If an organization doesn't offer such an opportunity, it is important for individuals to seek out ways to make this happen. To be considered for a promotion, individuals will benefit from advocating for both, a strong mentor and sponsor. They are equally necessary.

Data indicates that there is a strong need to mentor and sponsor other women. This will help women in the field gain the confidence necessary to seek job advancements. It also provides future leaders with an understanding of the importance of investing in individuals' professional development. May this practice be "paid forward" to future leaders within the workplace.

As you investigate places to work, it is important to study their culture. Research the statistics and understand the work environment, what is valued, and celebrated. If you're applying for a job advancement within your own organization, begin thinking how you can assist with the culture change, if needed.

It is time for organizations to expect women to apply for advancement and to positively support others, mentor, sponsor, and develop other women. Leaders that develop and implement strategies to support and sustain a healthy culture establish conditions for working women with family obligations, and those who have a strong mentoring, sponsorship program for *all* employees will attract more women leaders. These are the types of companies that are seen as progressive in today's environment.

In summary, career mapping is essential. Individuals that desire career advancement should keep an updated resume, understand situational leadership strategies and the importance of settings, seek out mentors and sponsors, invest in professional development that enhances skill deficits, and understand the importance of working and establishing a healthy work culture.

It will take both men and women to become accountable to change the paradigm and continue to break the disparity gap. Individuals and organizations should be striving to become culturally proficient leaders where problems aren't ignored, data is used to make decisions, and leadership skills are an activity, not a trait. It is time to understand that true leadership is about disrupting a system that produces unacceptable outcomes to achieve equality.

## PROBLEM-SOLVING SCENARIO

You have taught eight years in an elementary school and just received a master's degree in curriculum and supervision. You have served on a few committees but understand that you may need more experience. The job of your dreams, K–12 curriculum director, just opened up. You decide to apply and see where it goes. You end up making it to the top three finalists but don't get the position. The position goes to someone with more experience.

### Questions

1. What do you do to gain more experience?
2. How do you gain more exposure for future vacancies?
3. What items do you include in your curriculum vitae?

### Reflections

- Where do you want to be in the next five years?

- What experiences will be on your resume to display your interests?
- Who would you like to mentor you?
- What organizations can you join?

# Chapter 11

# Know Your Strengths

Don't be insecure if your heart is pure.—Lady Gaga

*Using the Strengths Within a Team Yields Better Results Than Using Individual Strengths Alone*

*Staff meetings should be a place to connect people and build trust. As a former principal, I saw these meetings as a time to build bridges. This was an opportunity to build the best staff by understanding the needs, using individual strengths, to build a "team" of doing what was best for children. Using this strategy helped build four staffs to become buildings of "best practice," schools that increase scores 10 to 20% over previous years' performance.*

*When reflecting upon past experiences, I always enjoyed the light bulb moment. I remember playing a revised game of Jeopardy on an oversized board. The visuals provided clarification of the plan and how the pieces fit together. It was such a thrill to see the staff understand the goal. The moment of learning is fun to observe, no matter the age.— Sandra Gail Bussell*

As a female, have you ever applied for a job advancement and the position went to another person? If so, was this person male? As a candidate interviewing for a position, it is acceptable to make an appointment with the interviewer to seek input on ways to enhance your interview skills.

Don't let the negativism of not securing the job get you down. It is best to adopt a "growth mindset" by taking a step back and reflecting on how to improve. Do your homework and know the strengths, skills you bring to the table, and those who can be enhanced by others.

It is important for people to understand that interviewing for a position is like trying on a new pair of shoes—it has to be a perfect fit. If
not, the discomfort will make it necessary to find a pair that feels good
or a work environment that is a better fit. It is also important to realize
when things aren't a good fit. This doesn't mean that one is a failure.
It just means that there is a better place that aligns more with your philosophy. Don't let the failure get you down. Pick yourself up until you
land in the right place.

Once you do the homework, knowing your skill sets and how you're
perceived in a formal interview, it will be time to develop your executive presence skills. When we don't get a position, sometimes it isn't
personal; it just may be the way we're perceived.

Recall in a prior chapter where *ABC News* showed a video clip on
gender bias while interviewing. The male and female used the exact
same words, yet they were viewed as extremely different. Statistics
show that 75% of the time, the executive role will go to a male. Is this
because most people would rather work for a male? Could this be how
women are perceived? Are women viewed as being unsupportive? The
outcome certainly causes some reflection. Rather than responding to
the lack of a promotion in a negative manner, consider developing an
executive presence.

The definition of *executive presence* is a set of behaviors seen as the
outcomes of how we act that creates an interpretation about our ability. Dr. Paul Aldo, author of *Understanding Executive Presence*, states,
"Executive presence is a persona that we project to others through our
behavior. It is the outcome of how we act (the way we stand and move,
our body image, and what we say, how we say it) and the way others
interpret and respond to our actions."[1]

If this is the case, what are the correct behaviors? Aldo writes that
there are nine categories of behavioral expression that show up in
executive presence evaluation. He labeled them the "Nine Expressive
Dimensions" and organized them into three groups. The first three, passion, poise, and self-confidence, are about how we present ourselves;
candor, clarity, and openness deal with how we communicate; and,
finally, thoughtfulness, sincerity, and warmth are about how we relate
with others.[2]

Reflecting upon this definition of executive presence, how do you
think others view you as a leader? When we think about behaviors, do

people see you as one who displays passion about the work? As a leader are you presenting yourself with poise and confidence? In the educational field this would be a strong leader that displays career ambition, a strong sense of mission, a drive for improved outcomes, and a sense of perseverance.

A strong leader that displays poise is seen as one who keeps a consistent composure during highs and lows. A person that is comfortable around a diverse group of people is seen as one who is savvy and displays organizational agility. Sometimes a display of strong self-confidence can be misunderstood. However, self-confidence is a leadership skill that is also admired. People want to follow those who are certain; those who have the ability to build relationships and somewhat work the room. Self-confidence is also described as a leader or coworker that is action oriented and can stand alone.

If passion, poise, or self-confidence is an area that causes discomfort, it is important to find one to two areas and create a plan of action to improve how you are perceived. This will increase your personal persona.

Within your organizations have you ever wondered how your team is perceived? When we are talking about the team, one thinks about how the team operates and communicates. Does your team communicate with candor, clarity, and openness?

Coworkers tend to admire those who have a knack for candor. Those who can openly inform their team of a negative message without degrading a person or the work of an organization. One who can be open, honest, personally disclose information, and have the ability to understand a multiple perspective. If one displays such strong skills, they have a tendency to have an ability to confront a direct report without being unprofessional or using a wicked tongue. These types of experiences will easily be perceived by the personal responses to the interview questions. People want to work for a leader that creates the conditions that support team productivity.

It is easier to follow those who display a sense of candor and clarity than those who say everything is great to your face, but learn differently from the rest of the team. When leaders can communicate with candor and clarity it helps manage the vision and allows the organization to understand the purpose of the work. This type of leader will have strong written and verbal communication skills.

Last, it is important to develop relationships. Are you taking times to know your people? Do you interact with sincerity, thoughtfulness, and warmth? If not, people tend to not trust the leader.

In summary, it is important to know your strengths, understand how your behavior as a leader is perceived through communication, and understand the importance of relationships. If there is a deficit that needs to be developed, don't let this get you down. Remember that behaviors can be changed. It requires focus, discipline, consistency, patience, and training. To build and sustain trust within the organization, consistency is a must.

## PROBLEM-SOLVING SCENARIO

You are a high school principal interviewing for a superintendent position. You apply in three districts. You are selected as one of two final candidates in all three school districts. In preparation for the first two final interviews, you go out and buy two new suits. You make an appointment to have your hair done prior to the big community interviews. After the final interviews you feel really good about the potential outcomes. You feel well prepared for the community interviews and your perception is that you were well received.

The following day, you learn that you aren't the final candidate. As much as you would have liked to work in the districts, you are still pleased that you had one additional interview. In preparation for the last interview for the final position, you consult with another female superintendent. After the consultation, you still feel mentally prepared; however, you learn that you may have selected the wrong suit and hairstyle. Thus, in the last final interview, you decide to wear a pantsuit instead of a skirt suit. You also put your hair in a bun instead of wearing it down.

You later learn that the board of education was offering you a superintendent contract for the district for which you interviewed last. You can't wait to go back and share the great news with your female mentor.

## Questions

1. Why was the third and final interview more successful than the first two final interviews?

2. Did the pantsuit and hairstyle make the difference?
3. Is this related to executive presence? Why? Why not?

## Reflections

- Do you display a growth mindset? How?
- What are your skill sets?
- What personal and/or group behaviors would you like to develop into a strength?
- How will you do this?

## NOTES

1. Paul Aldo. (2014). *Understanding Executive Presence*. Laurel, MS: Gin Press, 10.
2. Aldo, *Understanding Executive Presence*, 13.

# Chapter 12

# Know How to Negotiate

The success of every woman should be the inspiration to another. We should raise each other up. Make sure you're very courageous: Be strong, be extremely kind, and above all be humble.— Serena Williams

*Personal Stories About Women and Salaries*

*Story One*

*Since I began teaching, money has not been very important to me. I have significantly more discretionary income than my parents had, and my life is quite comfortable. In my first administrative role, assistant principal, my raise was about 50% of my teaching salary. Wow! In my second administrative role, principal in a new district, my raise was about 10% my first year, but after seeing my work, I received a 20% salary increase the next year. Once again changing districts for an assistant superintendent role, my first year's salary was an adequate increase, and a larger one followed the second year after they saw my work.*

*In my negotiation for a superintendent's salary, things started to falter. I followed a superintendent who had been in the district for more than ten years, so I expected to be offered less than he made. When the offer came in, I was so excited for the opportunity I accepted a substantially lower salary than the outgoing superintendent. There were some negotiations with the contract and the salary moved up a little, but I believed the board would see my good work and again my year two would be an equity adjustment based on my performance. Revenues have been pretty flat for the district, and although I received excellent performance reviews, the raises have not been excellent. I have shared salary studies that show comparable districts with less experienced superintendents who are making significantly more. The superintendents are all men. I have not found a successful argument to be paid what I believe I deserve. It isn't about the money, I don't need it, but I do believe I deserve it. Oddly enough, the one year I shared that I was too tired to argue for a raise, they rewarded me with double what the other administrators received.—Anonymous author*

*Story Two*

*It is so important to negotiate for your salary. Several decades ago, I accepted an elementary principal position in two different buildings. The following year, my sister accepted a principal position in one building in the very same school district. Although I had seven more years of experience and was responsible for two buildings, not one, my sister was brought in at a higher salary. This wasn't her fault. She did a better job negotiating. Ladies, it is imperative to negotiate your salary. It pays off to do your homework and understand your value.—Kelly Murray Spivey*

## THE IMPORTANCE OF NEGOTIATION

Good negotiations set a person up for success. When you receive an official salary package offer, it is important to assess and understand if this is the package you desire. Those who know what they want by preparing ahead of time and asking questions during this transition do a better job negotiating.

Think about this, if someone accepts an offer $10,000 less than their counterpart, this is $100,000 during a ten-year period. Is this worth it? It is also an expectation to provide employers with an action plan on how performance will increase under one's leadership. A 5 to 10% raise is a realistic bump depending on the job advancement. According to Hewitt Research, a 3.1% raise is an average raise during evaluation times. Women shouldn't fear to ask for a competitive salary within the market.

It is important to understand the market and salary comparisons, and not to sell yourself short when negotiating salary. People that do this best understand the needs of the position and how they contribute to the overall success of the organization. It is important to assess the situation and complete a needs assessment of company and individual worth.

Once a needs assessment of common interests is complete, it is time to prepare your request. Understanding the organization's needs, your net worth, and your value to the success of the organization will assist in providing a rationale for your request. It is important to understand that this information be combined with market comparisons. What are the salary comparisons with level of experience compared to your desired salary? As you are preparing for negotiations, it is also acceptable to prepare an action plan of what you hope to accomplish during the first year or two in the position. These elements will help create a comprehensive request.

It is acceptable to ask for the salary desired. Women that do this best understand that this is a two-way engagement process. When engaging it is important to not come off demanding but negotiate for all those in the household but yourself. Positive emotion during this engagement process is imperative. As you work through this process, understand your bottom line and how you add value to the overall success of the organization.

Last, it is time to collaborate on the final package. Remember that this is a two-way engagement process where both parties are discussing common interests and needs. Women do better when they understand the bottom line and aren't afraid to ask, but not demand. The key to the final stage of negotiations is to remain positive and be strong in negotiating on behalf of the family, not self.

In summary, women do a better job of negotiating their individual salary when they assess the market, know their needs and the organization's needs, ask for what they desire, and understand the bottom line when sealing the deal. It is important that women *do not* sell themselves short.

## PROBLEM-SOLVING SCENARIO

You are a newly appointed female CEO. You receive your first big contract only to learn that your written contract provides far less benefits and salary than the former CEO.

## Questions

1. What do you do? Why?

## Reflections

- What position do you desire in the future?
- What is the market value?
- Were men paid at the same level as women? If not, why?
- How will you ask for what you want?

# Chapter 13

# Leaving a Legacy

Yesterday is gone. Tomorrow has not come. We have only today. Let us begin.—Mother Teresa

*A Personal Story by Judy Holden Murray*

*Leaving a legacy: I knew I wanted to be a teacher since I was a little girl. I believe that the love and passion I displayed for this work impacted others. My younger sister and all three daughters followed my footsteps. Being an only child for generations to receive a college degree was a gift for me. The gift I felt was from God. The gift was that I knew I was destined to be a schoolteacher at a very young age.*

*When time came for college—1958—I realized you needed money. I asked my stepfather if he could help. His answer was it would be a waste of money because women just got married and had babies. Thankfully, my biological father's brother believed in an education for everyone. He had the money to pay for my college. I got married after a year of college but was determined to follow my dream. I began teaching at age nineteen with only two years of college. Three daughters and a master's degree later, I went into administration.*

*I didn't realize my path in life and my determination would impact my daughters' lives. Having the positivity of words and actions, the importance of having survival goals in life, and being a role model of hard work were impacting my children. Being a child of divorce, I was determined to have a solid family base and to be able to take care of myself if ever on my own and to pass this philosophy down to my children.*

Historically, there are many women who have stood out. Just a few of the greats include Harriet Tubman, Mother Teresa, and Oprah Winfrey. These strong women are examples of those who demonstrate love, compassion, and understanding, have gone against the odds to improve the lives of others, and are courageous when sharing their stories.

Who do you admire? Are there women that are living today or lived before you that you admire? What legacy do you want to leave? What is your story? Let's not leave our legacy to chance. Let's be mindful, focused, and model the attitude, mindset, and behaviors we want others to look up to.

Unlike the strong women who have left a legacy, many women are conditioned to ignore certain behaviors and events that contribute to the gender disparity within the workforce by not speaking up or ignoring the inappropriate behavior. This only perpetuates the problem. It is important to educate oneself, bring awareness to certain behaviors, and utilize one's voice to educate others in a respectful, professional manner. It is time for women to stand up and address some of the biases that have been discussed since the enlightenment era.

It is important to use one's voice to change behavior and understand institutionalized oppression, which allows those in the dominant culture to accrue privilege and benefits they may not even recognize.

How many times have you been in a professional setting where the woman speaking isn't heard? This will occur when women are talked over or a male interrupts to talk for their female colleague. It is believed that people from historically oppressed groups unknowingly or unwittingly continue the policies and practices that flow from the benefits of the privileged. The systematic exploitation of one social group by another for its own benefit involves institutionalized control on the oppressed group.

In an open, inclusive, relational organization, it is easier for an organization to adapt. Change occurs with a commitment to gain awareness, an understanding, and interactions that engage different cultures. These experiences will transform individuals into a productive, culturally proficient team member.

It is never too late to learn new behavior. Learning can occur at any age. It is time to stop ignoring inappropriate patterns that oppress. It is important to become an active listener and have an open mind to differences to improve the climate, culture, that directly impacts individual and group success. It is time to be the leader that others strive to be.

Once we educate ourselves on biases, we become aware and understand the need to change behaviors. As stated in the book *Culturally Proficient Leadership*, the culturally proficient leader uses the six stages to proficient practice. These stages include cultural destructiveness, cultural incapacity, cultural blindness, cultural precompetence, cultural competence, and cultural proficiency.[1]

When we allow others to act in cultural destructiveness, we are allowing individuals to use their own power to eliminate another's culture. This also perpetuates the problem, supporting a need for immediate change. When organizations are operating in the proficiency mode, they are aware, engaged, and more likely to interact with other cultures. It is everyone's job to understand the needs of diverse views and accept how we can change behavior toward a more equitable environment.

Why is it that men do a better job than women at sponsoring, mentoring, and coaching other men that demonstrate potential for advancement? Are women taught to compete with other women by nature? Just proposing this question and reflecting upon practice will create a change in personal behavior.

It is believed that throughout time, more change will occur with social justice issues (for example, disparity); however, it needs to be understood that everyone has accountability when it comes to these issues. Becoming active listeners, understanding that a proposed view may not be yours but it is one owned and valued by another person, learning to be open-minded, using voice to create perspective, and being okay with the fact that closure may not take place instantly will lead to progress.

It is necessary to teach our young children to have a voice, solve problems, and accept and value differences. This will take a conscious practice and willingness to accept the need to empower young girls and women. It is imperative that more women apply for the executive roles. Now is the time to take a stand and make systemic change for the future. It is time for individuals to think about the legacy they want to leave behind.

What will your legacy be? It is necessary to be courageous by continuing to support important causes, reflecting on what is personally important, sharing the blessings with others, being a mentor to others, and sharing your passion. Take a stand—your actions will be contagious.

## PROBLEM-SOLVING SCENARIO

Harriet Tubman was born into slavery in the early 1820s. She married twice and was a true leader in helping slaves find freedom. When she was twenty-nine years old, Harriet walked more than ninety miles to escape from slavery and gain her freedom. Within a ten-year period, she made approximately twenty trips, helping another three hundred slaves find their way to freedom. Tubman was bold and she displayed moral grit and drive. She certainly paved a courageous path for many women to follow.

### Questions

1. Do you think Harriet's attitude, behavior, and mindset were learned or innate?
2. Do you think that Harriet was scared to be a major conductor in the Underground Railroad?
3. Do you think Harriet put others before herself?
4. Do you think Harriet Tubman understood the impact she would make on generations to follow?

### Reflections

- What legacy do you want to leave?
- Do you actively engage others? Do you value differences? If so, how?
- Do you use your voice to improve things like behaviors, process, and communication?
- What changes do you want to see before you leave your current position? How will you accomplish this goal?

## NOTE

1. Raymond D. Terrell. (2018). *Culturally Proficient Leadership*, 2nd ed. Thousand Oaks, CA: Corwin.

# Conclusion

Use your voice to educate and help change your culture and the
world.—Kelly Murray Spivey

Some people may see the current statistics as outdated. This says a lot
about the topic. The statistics speak for themselves. Little improvement
on the appointment of female executives in the highest positions has
been made in the past seven decades. No change occurred from the
mid-1600s to mid-1900s. Only then did we see a movement within
women disparity. It has taken strong women to speak up and make a
mark for the others behind them. I think of many great women that have
walked this path. Many are listed in the header quotes of each chapter.
The question for you is, "Is this enough?" Are you pleased with the
outcomes? If not, what can you, as an individual, do to improve this
situation. It is up to personal choice to ignore or take a stand.

As a mother and former teacher, I believe there is a need to increase
females' confidence to accomplish personal desires and dreams. Often,
women blame themselves or others for not accomplishing their goals.
Also, as women, we often ignore certain behaviors and events that
contribute to the gender differences in the workforce by ignoring inappropriate behavior and not speaking up about observing attitudes and
behaviors. This only perpetuates the problem. It is important to educate
oneself, bring awareness to certain behaviors, and utilize one's voice to
educate others in a respectful, professional manner. It is time to address
some of the bias issues that have been discussed since the enlightenment era. If we don't begin using our voice and the personal skill sets
to change behavior, we promote institutionalized oppression, which

allows those in the dominant culture to accrue privilege and benefits that many may not even recognize.

Now is the time to quit informing little girls they are bossy. Let's tell them they are a strong leader while teaching them how to use their strength for maximum performance. This may eliminate the action of grown women ignoring rude behavior in others because they don't want to be seen as bossy. Instead, they can address personal deficits without putting others down to make themselves look better. It is also time to use our voice to respectfully address these problems. The message shouldn't be negative. Positive words can be used for others to understand oppression. Establishing ground rules makes it easy to address inappropriate behavior. One can say, "In respect to ground rules, let's refocus on the task." If the inappropriate behavior, attitude, or mindset pertaining to gender disparity occurs in public, it is suggested that a private conversation occur. After all, if nothing else, maybe you can make a friend from the experience.

Historically, people from oppressed groups unknowingly or unwittingly continue the policies and practices that flow from the benefits of the privileged. The systematic exploitation of one social group by another for its own benefit involves institutionalized control on the oppressed group.

Let's lead by example. The second woman appointed to the U.S. Supreme Court, Ruth Bader Ginsburg, fought decades of gender discrimination during her education and career. Her legacy is her passion, dedication, tenacity, and commitment toward women's rights. She led by example the importance of using her voice to make necessary changes on human rights issues. Justice Ginsburg said, "Real change, enduring change, happens one step at a time." Are you willing to take that step?

Change begins with you. When each individual is committed to change by their willingness to open their mind and heart to gain awareness about others, understand differences, and engage within other cultures, growth occurs. This allows one to transform into a culturally proficient member of a team or society. In an open, inclusive, relational organization, everyone adapts.

It is never too late to learn how to support one another's needs. Learning can occur at any age. It is time to stop ignoring inappropriate patterns that oppress others because we understand that the environment impacts learning and success.

Once you educates yourself on biases, you can become aware and understand the need to change behaviors. Implementing the cultural proficient leadership strategies provides a guide for institutionalized change. It is important for individuals to understand the needs of diverse views and accept how we are responsible to change individual behavior toward a more equitable environment.

Gender disparity is evident. Although people today are doing a better job teaching children to have a voice, become better problem solvers, and to value differences, there is still room for much improvement. This will take a conscious practice and willingness to accept the need to empower young girls and women. In this world, may everyone experience love, kindness, compassion, understanding, peace, success, and happiness. You truly have the ability to change the world! Let's begin this journey together. Let's leave a legacy that other women want to follow. The time to stand up is *now*.

# Resources

## ACTIVITY 1: WOMEN YOU MOST ADMIRE

**Supplies:** Paper, pencil, chart paper, markers
**Directions:**

1. On a piece of paper list three women who you most admire.
2. In a small group take turns sharing who you listed and why you listed them.
3. In a large group list the names and discuss.
4. Create a journal reflection about this activity.

**Large Group Questions:**

1. Who did you list? Pick a few names off the list and ask why they were listed?
2. Was this a difficult task? Why? Why not?
3. What strengths did these women display that are similar to your strengths?
4. What legacy would you like to leave?

**Outcome:** This activity may be difficult. Women typically don't think of other women as role models. This is a great reflective activity.

## ACTIVITY 2: QUEEN BEE CHECKLIST— ARE YOU A QUEEN BEE?

**Directions:** Review and respond to the following questions by calibrating your answer. 1 = not at all, 2 = somewhat, and 3 = most likely.

1. Do you expect more from others than yourself?  1    2    3
2. Do you participate in workplace gossip?    1    2    3
3. Do you want to be in control or in power at all times?  1    2    3
4. Do you refuse to help others by expecting them to learn new expectations on their own?  1    2    3
5. Do you lack confidence at work?    1    2    3
6. Do you participate in negativity toward others by starting the conversation or laughing, agreeing with another coworker's negativity?  1    2    3
7. Do you crave power?    1    2    3
8. Do you put down others by focusing on their weaknesses rather than their strengths?    1    2    3
9. Is it important for you to always get your own way?  1    2    3
10. Is it important for you to always be seen and heard?  1    2    3

**Response Scale:**

1–10: You're *not* a queen bee.
11–20: You're *most likely* a queen bee.
21–30: You're *are* a queen bee. It's time to develop an intervention plan.

## ACTIVITY 3: GROWTH MINDSET

**Directions:** Think about the next job you want to apply for and answer these questions.
**Questions:**

1. What job do you want to have in the next three years?
2. How will you make this happen?
3. What are your strengths?
4. What are your areas of focus?
5. Who can you seek out as a mentor and sponsor?

**Tasks:**

1. Create/update your resume.
2. Keep your resume current by updating annually.
3. Work with your mentor and sponsor on a regular basis.
4. Apply for the position and interview. *This is a great experience that leads to building confidence.*

# About the Author

**Kelly Murray Spivey** is a retired superintendent from southwest Ohio. She served as president of the Buckeye Association of School Administrators in 2016–2017. During this time only 24% of women served as superintendents in the United States. She also worked to resolve cultural and diversity issues in her community. She received the NAACP Award in 2018.